Effective
TV Product

D1550115

Third edition

Gerald Millerson

FOCAL PRESS

To my friends and colleagues of the Department of Radio-Television-Film, School of Communications and Theatre, Temple University, Philadelphia, Pa.

Focal Press
An imprint of Butterworth-Heinemann Ltd
Linacre House, Jordan Hill, Oxford OX2 8DP

 PART OF REED INTERNATIONAL BOOKS

OXFORD   LONDON   BOSTON
MUNICH   NEW DELHI   SINGAPORE   SYDNEY
TOKYO   TORONTO   WELLINGTON

First published 1976
Reprinted 1979, 1980, 1981
Second edition 1983
Reprinted 1984, 1985, 1987, 1989, 1991
Third edition 1993

British Library Cataloguing in Publication Data
Millerson, Gerald
    Effective TV Production. – 3Rev.ed. –
    (Media Manuals Series)
    I. Title II. Series
    791.450232

ISBN 0 240 51324 X

Library of Congress Cataloguing in Publication Data
Millerson, Gerald.
    Effective TV production/Gerald Millerson. – 3rd ed.
    p. cm. – (Media Manuals)
    Includes bibiographical references.
    ISBN 0 240 51324 X
    1. Television – Production and direction. I. Title. II. Series.
    PN1992.75.M48 1993
    791.45'0232–dc20   92–37229
                                                             CIP

Phototypeset by Deltatype Ltd, Ellesmere Port, Cheshire
Printed and bound in Great Britain

m media MANUAL

Contents

Introduction to the third edition

This long-established introductory workbook has been extensively revised to meet today's productional needs. It has been specially designed to give you an immediate overview of television/video production fundamentals in a concise, easily digested form. You will find outlined here the proven methods and techniques that underlie persuasive program-making.

You will meet the principles and practices of various crafts, and the contributions they make towards the final presentation.

Whether television/video production is your main study, or part of a media course, whether you will be working with a single video camera or a multi-camera team, you will find encapsulated here the essentials of effective production techniques. These basics will provide you with a firm foundation for later experience.

Terms vary between organizations, but you will find the commonest included here. More detailed studies of the medium in the author's other titles are listed at the end of this book.

Where the convention of the masculine gender is more widely understood internationally, it has been used in this text; although, of course, both women and men carry out all the jobs discussed.

Acknowledgment

The author would like to thank the Director of Engineering of the British Broadcasting Corporation for permission to publish the original book.

Television today

For all practical purposes, you can regard *television* and *video* as identical media. They involve the same skills, equipment and techniques.

Broadly speaking, while *television* usually transmits programs direct to the general public (via broadcast transmitters, cable or satellite), *video* is invariably concerned with non-broadcast or *closed-circuit* material.

However, even that distinction is becoming increasingly blurred. We find that programs originally made for 'video' audiences are frequently broadcast, and 'television' programs are now widely marketed for home viewing.

The scale of operations

Television and video programs today are made by production units ranging from a single person with a camcorder, to a large group of specialists with a multi-camera team. Equipment varies from basic to state-of-the-art.

While some organizations have their own fully fitted studios and go-anywhere mobile units for *remotes/outside broadcasts*, others hire equipment as needed from facility houses, to suit particular program needs.

Some program makers work mainly *on location* – in streets, public buildings, hired halls, houses, the countryside, etc. Others are usually based in regular *TV studios*, where built scenery provides backgrounds to their productions.

Originally, broadcast organizations produced most of their programs in-house. Today, an increasing number are 'buying in' complete programs from freelance production groups. Some stations are mainly involved with transmitting videotaped or filmed programs prepared by others.

Live or taped

Whether a TV program is being transmitted *live* or recorded on *videotape* can have a major influence on production techniques.

In a *live production*, your audience sees the actual events as they are happening. They feel that they are watching through the camera's eye, and there is always the thrill of the unexpected! This can add to the tension, and excitement of the occasion, especially in a sporting event, where the results are not known.

For many program subjects, however, the advantages of 'seeing it live' are arguable. Certainly, for the production team, live transmission can be restrictive. When we watch a good taped or filmed production, there is still a sense of *immediacy*, an illusion of realism. We quickly become engrossed, even where we know the outcome, or realize that the performers are no longer living.

Recording a program on *videotape* gives the director an extra productional dimension. There is greater flexibility, a freedom to correct and modify, to produce a more polished eye-catching product. The production process itself is simplified in many ways. And, most important, you end up with a product that can be marketed, or retained as archive material for inserts into future programs. An unrecorded live production is lost for ever.

TELEVISION
Propagated by
BROADCAST TRANSMITTERS – SATELLITE – CABLE
for
PUBLIC BROADCASTS

Newscasts Weather Sport Interviews

Drama Documentary Music Science

Films Comedy Adventure Hobbies

Wildlife Talks Dance Children

Game shows Demonstrations Talk shows

etc.

VIDEO
Propaged by
VCR CASSETTES – SATELLITE – CABLE
For individual, carrel, or group viewing ...
in home, study center, workplace,
training center, library, seminar,
sales point, exhibition, etc.

Box-shaped (deep), handle flat on top
controls visible as shown
SEPARATE LOUDSPEAKER UNIT with 'sound'

Home entertainment
Hobbies
Home instruction

Product information
Public relations

Study/Education
Instruction/Training
Troubleshooting

Self-assessment
Critiques

Displays
Demonstrations
Sales promotions

Conferences/group address
Staff coordination
Overflow meetings

Hobbies
Group projects

Television Production

Television production is often a carefully balanced compromise between artistic aspirations and hard practicalities.

On the one hand there are the less tangible 'artistic' aspects of the program. The *way* you present ideas will influence how your audience receives and interprets them. The way you use your camera(s), intercut successive shots, arrange lighting and sound, will give the subject itself a certain authenticity. Poor or inappropriate presentation can trivialize it.

On the other hand, we must never forget such down-to-earth matters as cost, time, space, facilities, personnel required, etc. It is not surprising that decisions are often a choice between conflicting issues.

Opportunities and limitations

In practice, you will find that a number of factors directly influence how you present a subject, and the techniques you decide to use.

Where, for instance, you are shooting an event that has been arranged by others, you may be able to plan your general approach, but will often have to adapt techniques to suit conditions as you find them. In these circumstances, there are seldom opportunities for 'retakes' or 'repeat action'. So you have to rely on subsequent editing to hide faults and omissions.

In the empty studio, you seem to have free choice to arrange the entire action and production treatment to get exactly the effects you want. You have complete control over everything that is happening – theoretically, at least! The drawback of this 'blank sheet' situation is that, until you have planned and organized the program, you have nothing to shoot!

While many program subjects can be shot at any time, others are more restrictive. For example, you may have to wait for the right season to see plants in bloom, or go to a suitable location to find the snow required in the story line.

Some situations give plenty of opportunity to select shots at leisure. Others are one-time opportunities, where you need an instinct for 'the right moment'.

Some types of action are concentrated in a limited area (e.g. snooker table), while other activities are spread out over a broad field (e.g. marathon runs, ski events).

Style

As you will see, productional treatment can range from a straightforward presentation, to a highly stylized form.

Production may be primarily a matter of *organization*; bringing the right elements together (script, performers, settings, etc.) and using cameras and microphones to display the performance through carefully selected shots.

At the other extreme, production can be a *persuasive process*, in which you carefully arrange picture and sound to influence your audience in particular ways, to play on their emotions.

TYPICAL FACTORS THAT INFLUENCE PRODUCTION METHODS

How you present a subject and organize your facilities can depend on the program subject and the audience:

The nature of the subject
- Some program topics require considerable preparation, e.g. research, specialist knowledge, finding suitable illustrations, etc.
- Even a straightforward presentation may involve extensive organization – re copyright, insurance, technical problems.
- Some subjects pose inherent problems, e.g. children, animals, materials that quickly deteriorate.

The program format
- Some presentations follow established routines (e.g. interviews); and an entirely different approach may prove unacceptable or distracting.

The type of presentation
- Some subjects require special facilities or preparation (e.g. models, computer graphics).
- If the program is to be based on borrowed/hired material (e.g. library film), is this available?
- Some types of production (e.g. dance, moving vehicles) need a lot of space to be presented effectively.

Program emphasis
Is the main aim of your program:
- To amuse and entertain your audience?
- To inform them (e.g. provide data, instruct, guide)?
- To teach (e.g. language course)?
- To persuade them to buy or use a product (sales, advertising)?
The productional approach will depend on the program's purpose.

The audience
- Is your audience 'captive' or 'casual'? Do you need to grab attention to persuade them to watch (advertisement), or are they eager and attentive (cooking demonstration)?
- Is the program subject familiar to them, or is it a new and complicated topic?
- Are there likely to be problems with terminology or language?

Audience viewing conditions
- Will the audience be close or distant from the TV screen(s)? Will detail be clearly discernible?
- Are individuals watching in their own homes (distractions), at a study carrel, a group seminar?
- Can they watch the program tape over and over, or is it one-time presentation?

The duration of the presentation
- The duration of the presentation will affect how many topics/themes you can cover, how far you can develop ideas.
- Is it a single complete presentation, or one of a series? Are parts self-contained, or related to (developed from) others?

Live or recorded presentation
- Is the program being presented 'live', 'live-on-tape', or edited?
- Are there opportunities for retakes to correct and improve?
- Will editing involve basic compilation, or full post-production treatment?

Production conditions
- Will the program be *studio-based* or *on location* (i.e. self-dependent)?
- Single-camera or multi-camera approach?
- Is it to be unrehearsed, or partially or fully rehearsed?
- Will it be recorded straight through, or in sections?

13

The Production Team

- *Executive producer.* Overall production head. Controls/coordinates business management, budget, group organization, administration, policies, etc.

- *Producer.* Organizes/oversees specific production.

- *Director.* Interprets and stages production, guiding/coordinating operations.

- *Assistant/associate director (AD)/production assistant (PA).* Aide supervising on director's behalf (may help cuing, timing, set up shots).

- *Producer's assistant (script asst).* Checks/timing, performance against script; notes problems; liaison, cues, etc.

- *Production manager.* Aids producer/director, checking budget costings.

- *Floor manager/floor director (stage manager).* Director's aide in studio, cuing/guiding performers, conveying instructions. General studio organization. (Assisted by assistant floor manager.)

- *Writer/scriptwriter.* Creates/develops script.

- *Researcher.* Fact-finds subject background.

- *Script editor.* Assesses/guides script form.

- *Talent* seen on camera includes: actors, performers/artistes, musicians, singers, dancers, announcers, interviewers, emmcees (MCs), anchors, newscasters, guests, contestants, audience.

- *Technical director/studio (remote) supervisor/technical coordinator/engineering manager/technical manager.* Coordinates/organizes technical facilities.

- *Camera crew (under senior cameraman).*

- *Camera operators/cameramen.* Operate video cameras.

- *Camera assistant/dolly operators/trackers/grips.* Aid camera operators (push dollies, guide cables).

- *Switcher/vision mixer.* Operates production switcher (Switching/mixing between video sources; basic video effects).

- *Lighting director/lighting designer.* Designs, arranges, controls lighting treatment.

- *Lighting assistant.* Assists with lighting arrangement and control.

- *Electricians/sparks* under *gaffer* or *chargehand.* Set up/adjust lighting equipment; operate lighting effects/cues.

- *Video operator/vision control operator/shader/video engineer.* Adjusts/controls camera equipment for optimum picture quality/matching.

- *Audio engineer/audio control/sound supervisor/sound mixer.* Controls technical/artistic quality of program sound. Assisted by sound crew.

- *Boom operator.* Operates sound boom or fishpole, positioning its microphone for best sound quality.

- *Audio operator/sound assistant.* Arranges and operates audio equipment (mikes, tape recorders, CDs, etc.).

- *Titling and graphics* prepared by *graphic artist, character generator operator, computer graphics artist.*
- *Video effects designer.* Creates and operates electronic video effects.
- *Set designer/scenic designer.* Conceives, designs, organizes scenic treatment.
- *Draughtsman.* Assists, prepares design plans/elevations, etc..
- *Set construction.* By *carpenters, painters,* etc. constructing/preparing scenery to designer's scheme.
- *Properties.* Hire/purchase/construction of items to furnish/decorate settings.
- *Set erection* (by *set crew*). Erect/build settings.
- *Set dressing* (by *stage crew*). Position properties/furniture/drapes.
- *Set decoration* (by *scenic artists*). Additional set decoration (e.g. floors).
- *Floor crew.* General aides moving scenery/props, etc., during show. (Called *stage hands/facilities men/floor men/scenic operatives.*)
- *Makeup designer.* Designs makeup treatment for larger production.
- *Makeup artist/makeup assistant.* Prepares and applies makeup treatment for talent.
- *Hairdresser/hair stylists.* Prepares/arranges hairwork for talent.
- *Costume designer.* Designs/selects/organizes clothing to be worn by actors/performers in larger production.
- *Wardrobe supervisor.* Arranges/organizes clothing in production.
- *Dresser/wardrobe handler.* Aids talent in fitting/dressing.
- *Special effects designer.* Designs and operates mechanical effects (e.g. rain, snow, fire, explosions).
- *Videotape (VTR) operator.* Operates equipment recording/reproducing TV picture/sound on magnetic tape.
- *VT editor.* Selects/arranges videotaped material for optimum effect. ('Off-line' and 'on-line' editing.)
- *Film channel/telecine operator.* Operates equipment reproducing film as TV picture/sound.
- *Post-production work.* Final editing, integration and adjustment of picture and audio sources into final videotape. (Adding music, effects, video effects, titles, 'Audio sweetening'.) Carried out by video, audio, VTR experts above.

The Director's Role

The TV director's job can vary between organizations, and with the type of production. The director is often totally responsible for *all* aspects of the show – from the initial idea, right through to the finished tape. In other setups, the director is primarily concerned with *interpreting and presenting* the program material, while a *producer* deals with its organization and administration.

Whatever the job emphasis, the director is always the key figure in the production team, guiding, co-relating and unifying their efforts.

The director's task
As you would expect, different types of production make their own particular demands on the director. In some, the director has continually to make off-the-cuff decisions, split-second selections, anticipatory moves: presenting events clearly; missing no important action.

Shooting a sports event, the director arranges camera viewpoints to give the best coverage, but has to rely on instant choice and a certain amount of luck for the maximum effect.

In a game show, the director provides a carefully prearranged framework for the action; but is ready to switch to catch the unexpected reaction.

In other types of production, every moment has been systematically planned. Camera and sound are used as persuasive tools; to conjure a particular mood or atmosphere, to direct and influence the audience's responses. In a drama production, the director carefully analyzes the script, and envisions how it can be presented to create a sympathetic and interesting interpretation of the text.

Then there are the types of production, such as newscasts and magazine programs, where the director's role is to provide and control a presentational framework; to present a series of separate items or 'stories' that have been developed by a team of researchers, journalists, etc.

The director's approach
There are two extreme ways in which directors work:
- *The selective approach*. Here, having developed and organized the production format, the director mainly relies on the team to contribute their particular expertise; e.g. camera operators offering the most effective shots. The setting and the lighting treatment are created by their respective experts.

The director assesses their contributions, and suggests any changes. But for the most part he/she concentrates on action, performance, shot development, switching. When controlling a fast-moving live production, this approach may be the most practical.
- *The director as the originator*. Here the director plans the production in great detail, and relies on the team to follow these specifications, and bring these ideas to life. Guided by the director's ideas about settings, picture composition, etc., they organize and arrange the mechanics to translate these decisions into material form.

In practice, of course, we find something of each of these approaches in everyday production.

The director's job has many facets!

Analysis
- Assessing program ideas
- Building them into a coherent theme
- Considering how to present that theme
- Judging its effectiveness

Explanation
- Describing program concepts to the production team

Consultation/technical planning
- Checking methods, techniques, equipment, staging, safety, regulations, etc.

Organization
- Arranging budget, services, personnel, casting/booking talent, booking facilities, etc.
- Productional paperwork (scripts, order forms, booking, etc.)

Preparation
- Arranging contributory items (e.g. titling, graphics, video effects, music, library/stock inserts)

Guidance (during planning, rehearsal, recording)
- Guiding talent/performers (*re* positions, moves, timing, delivery, etc.)
- Guiding team (*re* shots, switching, sound, lighting, setting, graphics, costume, makeup, etc.)
- Selecting, modifying, suggesting changes
- Cuing (talent, action, movement, switching, etc.)
- Rationalizing (resolving operational/staging problems)

Coordinating
- Contributory services (videotape and film channels)

Evaluating
- Checking artistic values (e.g. performance, pace)
- Checking action, dialogue/lines
- Checking camerawork (e.g. framing)
- Checking durations of sequences/program
- Assessing needs for retakes, or alterations

Editing
- Off-line editing (determining editing/changes/treatment needed)
- On-line editing (guiding/assessing post-production editing)

Publicity
- Organizing/contributing publicity material

TV Camera Units

Television/video production groups use a number of different camera arrangements – from a single camera unit, to a complex multi-camera setup.

Single camera units

Here the production is shot with a single walkabout video camera. For briefer takes, this generally rests on the operator's shoulder. Otherwise it is attached to some form of mounting – typically a tripod.

For *sound pickup*, a microphone fitted to the camera may be used. But for higher quality and better positioning, a separate microphone is preferable – often on a *fishpole* held by another operator.

Picture and sound can be:

• *Recorded as in a camcorder*, on a video cassette recorder (VCR) that is either inbuilt, or attached to the camera.

• *Recorded on a separate portable VCR* (shoulder pack, back-pack, small cart/trolley).

• *Routed to a nearby vehicle*, using cable or a small transmitter (microwave, infrared). There the program is recorded on a VCR, or transmitted onwards to a remote pickup point.

For greater mobility, the camera operator can shoot from a moving vehicle – car, truck, motorcycle, helicopter . . . And then there are those improvised facilities, from ski-lift to hospital gurney!

Multi-camera units

Particularly when transmitting live programs, two or more cameras are often needed to give greater productional flexibility. Several standard arrangements are widely used:

Remotes van – Cameras are connected to lightweight video equipment via long cables. Other facilities may include a basic switcher, picture/sound control and monitoring, sound and videotape recorders.

Mobile control room/location production unit – This large custom-built truck or trailer provides a full broadcast standard production control center, with complete video and audio equipment. The unit can be used in several ways:

• Located at the scene of the action, with cameras and sound cables extended to their various operating positions.

• Its camera and audio equipment may be removed and relocated within a building to form a temporary control room (e.g. at a large-scale event in a sports stadium, or a conference center).

• It may include a small studio suitable for localized action, e.g. interviews.

Permanent studio – A regular installation, in which *cameras* are cabled to their associated video equipment (via wall outlets), and routed to a production switcher in the control room. *Studio microphones* are cabled into the audio equipment, and routed to an audio control board, where sources are selected and adjusted.

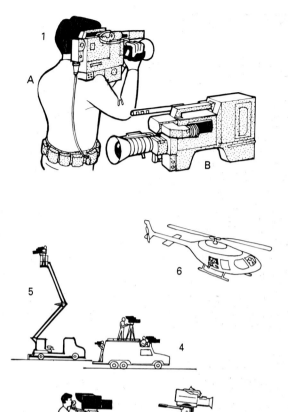

TV camera units
1. The lightweight camera (A) and camcorder (B). (Powered from a battery belt.)
2. The studio camera, mounted on a tripod. 3. Lightweight camera, mounted on a
pneumatic lightweight tripod. 4. Mobile van with hatch, roof, rear-platform
cameras. 5. Hydraulic platform. 6. Helicopter.

A Studio Tour

Whatever their size, most TV studios have a similar basic form.

Studio features

Considerable care and know-how go into successful studio design. Careful acoustical treatment of the walls and ceiling suppresses random echoes and reflected sounds. The level smooth floor surface allows quiet judder-free camera movement. A silent powerful air conditioning system maintains a comfortable working temperature.

Most of the studio floor is marked out as the *staging area (setting area)* – apart from a *safety lane/fire lane* around its edges, which is left free for easy access. Here all the *action* (performance) takes place within prefabricated *settings or sets*. These may be augmented by large cloths, drapes or scenic units hung from overhead support rails (scenic battens).

In small studios, most *lighting fittings* are attached to an overhead *pipe grid* or to *ceiling tracks*. Larger studios use a series of overhead *battens/barrels/bars* to suspend lamps. Other lamps may be supported on telescopic *floor stands*, or rest on the ground. The direction, coverage and brightness of each lamp is carefully adjusted to create an appropriate technical and artistic effect.

Around the studio walls, various services are available, including: power supplies, camera cable outlets, lighting and scenic hoist controls, mike points.

TV cameras

Most studios have two or three cameras mounted on wheeled dollies (usually *rolling tripods* or *pedestals*). Each has a long cable linking it, via a wall outlet, to a camera control unit (CCU) in a nearby 'apparatus room'. This two-way cable carries various supplies, synchronizing pulses, intercom, etc., and the picture signal (*video*) from the camera. After adjustment by a *video engineer (shader, video operator)*, each camera's picture is routed to a *production switcher (vision mixer)* in the nearby *production control room*. Here the director and his team sit, selecting from cameras' shots and other picture sources (videotape, film, slides, etc.).

Support areas

Larger studios usually have a nearby storage area where scenery and props can be held in transit. Another room may store various operational equipment, including lighting fittings, cameras, sound boom, picture monitors, loudspeakers, to leave the studio floor clear while settings are being built. Other facilities may include makeup and dressing rooms, etc.

A STUDIO TOUR

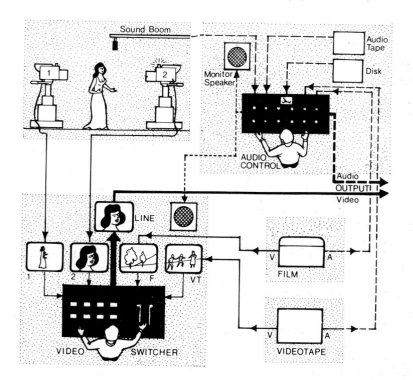

The TV studio system
This simplified diagram shows how video and audio sources are routed to their respective selection points.

21

Production Control

The *production control area* is the operations center of the TV show. Here in a room(s) overlooking the studio, the director and various members of the team select and control the program's pictures and sound sources.

Typical features

- *A bank of 'preview' or 'channel' picture monitors* continuously displays pictures from each video source: camera channels, film (telecine), videotape, slides, remotes, titles, etc.
- *A production switcher/vision mixer* which enables the director to cut/fade/mix between these picture sources – sending the selected channel(s) to line, to be recorded or transmitted. The equipment may be operated by the director, a specialist 'switcher', or the technical director. The switcher's selected output is displayed on the *line monitor/master monitor*.
- *Intercom (production talkback) circuits* allow the director to give the crew instructions, cues and guidance over their headphones without being overheard by studio microphones. (A loudspeaker is available in the studio, for any general announcements, but these are usually made by the FM.)
- *Monitor loudspeakers* in the production control room reproduce the program sound.
- *Sound desk.* Here all the program sound sources are selected, controlled and interblended (microphones, audio tapes, CDs/disks, videotape and film sound, etc.).
- *Video control.* The 'shader'/'video operator' adjusts the cameras' electronics and matches the picture quality from different sources.
- *Lighting console.* Here the production lighting is switched, and relative intensities balanced.
- *Videotape channel.* The program's picture and sound may be videotaped and replayed on local equipment, or in a separate area.
- *Film (telecine) channel.* Here standard 16 mm/35 mm film is replayed.
- *Slide scanner.* Apparatus for reproducing standard photographic slides. (These may be stored digitally in an 'electronic stills store (ESS)'.)
- *Character generator.* computer system for producing titles.
- *Graphics generator.* Computer system for producing graphical material (maps, graphs, etc.).
- *Special effects generator (SEG)*, providing wipes, visual effects, backgrounds etc. directly or by manipulating picture images. (May be part of the switcher equipment.)

Control room layout

Many organizations use a communal open-plan layout for production facilities; preferably with sound control in another room.

Large studios may have separate rooms for sound, lighting/video control, videotape, film, etc. Then instead of everyone wearing headsets for a communal intercom system, the director's separate intercom is heard over local loudspeakers, while private-wire circuits communicate between rooms.

22

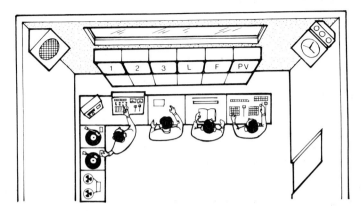

The 'communal' production control room

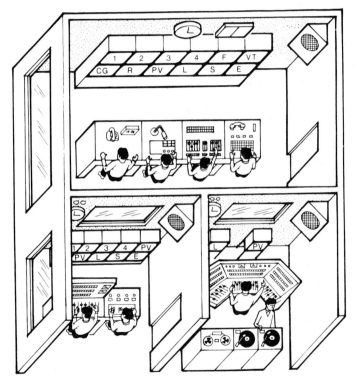

The 'sectionalized' production control room

23

The TV/Video Camera

TV/video cameras range from lightweight hand-held versions to large heavy-duty units. Some are more automated, or have more 'bells and whistles', than others. Although camera design directly affects picture quality (i.e. color fidelity, stability, tonal range, detail resolution, etc.), even more modest units now provide very satisfactory results.

While earlier cameras were built as completely integrated units, many of today's modular designs allow you to choose features to suit your particular shooting conditions.

The camera head
Basically, the 'camera' consists of:
- The *camera head* which contains its main electronics; including the image sensor that generates the picture.
- A suitable *lens system* (usually some form of *zoom lens*) fixed onto its front.
- A *viewfinder* attached to its top.
- A *power pack* or a small *videotape recorder (VCR)* may be fastened to the rear of a stand-alone camera.

Main features
An increasing number of electronic cameras now use solid-state *CCD image sensors* to generate the picture, instead of *camera tubes*. Both can produce excellent pictures, but the former have increasing practical advantages.

The TV camera system needs various power supplies, scanning and synchronizing pulses etc. to function:
- If you are using a stand-alone shoulder-mounted camcorder on location, these will be provided within the camera head.
- Alternatively, as in a multi-camera studio setup, they may be supplied via a camera cable, from a distant *camera control unit.*

While pictures from the stand-alone camera depend on preset or automatic adjustments, the cabled camera can be remotely adjusted by a specialist operator (shader, video control) to continuously maintain optimum picture quality and matching.

Cameras can usually be switched from single to multi-camera working. Then they are mutually synchronized by a central *genlock* system.

The zoom lens systems
Zoom lens systems are particularly complex. Where you want the highest optical quality, maximum light-gathering power, and a wide zoom range (i.e. max. to min. coverage) larger heavier lens systems are unavoidable. But where cameras are to be carried around, more compact zoom lenses are essential.

Types of viewfinder
To focus and compose shots accurately, you need a good viewfinder. This can take three often interchangeable forms:
- A small magnified (1.5 in/38 mm) monochrome picture tube, held up to the eye.
- A 5–7 in (12.5–18 mm) open-screen display with a light-hood.
- A clip-on LCD color screen (liquid crystal display).

24

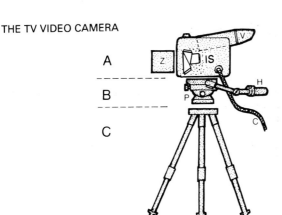

The television camera

The TV camera consists of:

A. The camera head   Z, zoom lens. IS, image sensors (CCDs). V, viewfinder.
C, camera cable (taking technical supplies to the camera, and the resultant video
to the camera control unit/CCU). A quick-release *wedge-mount* under the head
slides into a corresponding recessed plate on the panning head.

B. The panning head (pan head)   This enables the camera head to tilt and turn
(*pan*) smoothly. These movements can be restrained by deliberately introduced
friction (*drag*), and can be *locked off* to hold the head rigid. *Tilt balance* positions
the head horizontally, preventing it being nose- or tail-heavy. One or two attached
pan (*panning*) *handles* (H) enable the cameraman to direct and control the camera
head.

C. The camera mounting   This can take many forms, e.g. camera-clamp,
monopod, tripod, pedestal, crane.

25

Camera Controls

The controls and facilities you need on a camera really depend on how you are going to use it. For instance, while a news cameraman may welcome automatic circuits that prevent the picture from being accidentally over- or underexposed, in the studio, this problem is more effectively handled by the shader/video control operator at a central control unit.

Camera adjustments

There are several ways in which you can control the camera's picture:
- Altering the zoom's *lens angle* – By turning a ring on the lens barrel; or a control on a pan bar; or switches ('shot box', rocker switch). This will vary the lens' focal length, and adjust:

    How much of the scene appears in the shot (*coverage/field of view*).

    The apparent relative proportions/sizes of subjects at different distances (*perspective*).

    The relative sharpness of subjects at different distances (*depth of field.*)

    If you alter the lens angle while on shot, this produces the familiar *zooming* effect.
- *Focusing* – You adjust the distance at which subjects appear sharpest; by turning a ring on the lens barrel, or a control on a pan bar. How critical focusing is, depends on the lens angle, and the subject distance.
- Adjusting *exposure* – By turning an *f-stop* ring on the lens barrel (directly or by remote control). This changes the aperture of the lens iris, to alter the brightness of the lens image falling onto the camera's image sensor.

    This causes all picture tones to lighten or darken. (The lightest or the darkest may merge ('crush out') and lose modeling if the lens aperture is wrongly adjusted.) You can use *auto-iris* circuits used to control exposure automatically – but rather arbitrarily.
- *Video gain (boost)* – You can switch in extra amplification to strengthen the picture (video) when working in low light conditions. (This does not affect the overall *exposure* of the shot, and can increase picture noise ('snow').)
- *Color quality* – You can compensate for variations in the color quality of prevailing light (e.g. daylight, tungsten light) by switching in color filters or adjusting camera circuits (relative color gain).

Camera movements

You can move the camera to adjust its viewpoint by:
- *Panning* and *tilting*. Turning the camera head left/right or up/down.
- *Dollying/tracking*. Moving the camera to/from the subject or scene.
- *Trucking/crabbing* sideways.
- *Arcing* round it.
- *Elevating/depressing* ('ped-up'/'ped-down'). Raising/lowering the camera height.

26

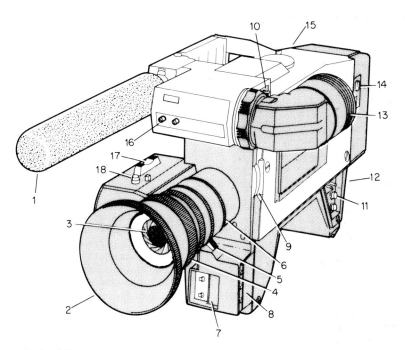

Parts of the camera

Camera designs vary, but the following are typical facilities found in the video camera:

1 Microphone – electret unidirectional
2 Lens hood
3 Lens aperture (iris) – f/1.6 max.
4 Focus control
5 Manual zoom control
6 Aperture control
7 White balance adjust; black adjust
8 Video gain (0 dB, 6 dB, 12 dB), color bars, camera standby/operate switch
9 Color compensation filter – 3200 K, 5600 K, 5600 K + 12.5% ND, closed
10 Viewfinder adjustable – 1.5 in (37 mm) with LED indicators
11 Power selection, intercom, audio monitoring jack
12 Camera back. VTR connector, video output camera cable, monitor video output, gen-lock connection for multi-camera setups
13 Eyepiece
14 Snap-on battery pack
15 Side of camera: mike input connector, external d.c. socket
16 Viewfinder controls
17 Power zoom switch
18 Auto-iris on/off

27

Camera Facilities

Camera facilities vary with design, but many are universal.

The camera lens

Most electronic cameras are fitted with a *zoom lens*. This can be adjusted to any coverage angle within its range; e.g. from 60° to 10° (a 6 to 1 ratio; 6:1). If this variation is insufficient, your options are:

- Fit a *different* zoom lens system. Designs of up to 44:1 are available.
- Clip on a *supplementary lens* or add an *adaptor ring.*
- Some zoom lenses include an *extender lens/range extender*, which can be flipped in/out to select two different ranges.

On a shoulder-mounted camera, the operator reaches round (left hand) to adjust the *focus* (distance), the *f-stop (iris, aperture)*, and the manual *zoom control* (lever on barrel-ring). The right hand supports the camera, with fingers on a rocker-switch controlling motorized zooming.

When the camera is fixed onto a *mounting*, both focus and zoom systems are usually extended by cable, to separate controls on the pan bars/panning handles, for easier access. In larger camera units, focus may be controlled by a knob at the right side of the camera head.

Many cameras have the choice of manual focusing, or '*autofocus*' (automatic focusing), which self-adjusts the lens for maximum sharpness.

The viewfinder

Adjustments to viewfinder controls (e.g. brightness, contrast) do not affect the camera's picture output. To make exact focusing easier, an inbuilt magnifier effectively enlarges the picture and electronic '*crispening*' circuits emphasize edge contrast.

Viewfinders may be switchable, to allow another camera's picture to be superimposed (to match shots), or to display technical test patterns (e.g. color bars) when checking the system's performance.

Indicators

Various *indicators* may be provided on the viewfinder (lights, meters, on-screen displays) which give the camera operator information about the system. Typically these include. 'on-air (cue-light)' or 'recording' (tally) light, white balance, backlight correction, battery alarm, boost setting, low light warning, shutter speed, video level (exposure).

Additional indicators may give information about the attached videotape recorder: low battery alarm, tape end warning, playback/recording, elapsed/remaining time.

Further indicators may be provided outside, on the sides and rear of the camera.

Audio

The camera operator's headset has an intercom mike, and may be fed with program sound in one earpiece, while the other provides *general intercom/talkback* and a private-wire intercom to the video engineer/video control, or the technical director.

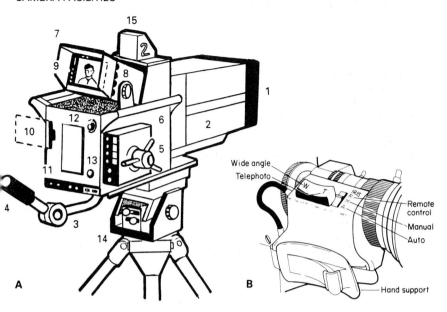

A

B

A The camera head

1 Lens hood (sun shade, ray shade)
2 Zoom lens
3 Adjustable panning handle (pan handle, pan bar)
4 Twist-grip zoom control
5 Focus control (many camers use a control mounted on a panning handle – RHS)
6 Shot box (mounted on the camera head, or on a panning handle – RHS)
7 Monochrome viewfinder (perhaps with magnifying lens)
8 Viewfinder controls (including hi-peaker, crispening image detail)
9 Indicators mimic tally light, lens-aperture indicator (f-stop), zoom lens setting (focal length/lens angle), etc
10 Camera card clip
11 Headset jack points (intercom and program) with volume controls. Mixed viewfinder feeds switch
12 Zoom lens range-extender switch
13 Call button (contacts shader/video control)
14 Camera mounting head (panning head/pan head) with drag adjustment for tilt and pan action, and tilt/pan locks. Also tilt fore-aft balance adjustment
15 Tally light with camera number, illuminated when camera selected to line on switcher.

B Focal length (lens angle) may be adjusted manually (zoom lever on lens barrel), or with a motor system (*power zoom*) operated by a rocker-switch from wide angle to telephoto (narrow angle). Nearby switches also control the lens *aperture (iris)* auto, manual, remote control.

29

Supporting the Camera

Although a lightweight camera can be hand-held or rested on the shoulder, if you are going to hold a shot for some time, or zoom in close, you really need some additional support to keep the picture steady. Several types and designs of camera mountings are available, each with its particular advantages and limitations.

Hand-held cameras
You can steady a hand-held camera with various devices:
- A *body-brace* (resting on the chest, or in a belt).
- A *monopod* or *tripod* for ground support.
- A special *stabilizing device* which compensates optically or electronically for camera shake.
- A '*Steadicam*' stabilizer unit, which steadies the camera, even when running and climbing.

The pan head/panning head
This fastens the camera to its mounting, and provides a pivot that allows it to be panned and tilted precisely, or 'locked off' firmly at any angle.

One or two *pan bars/panning handles* fixed to this head are used to point and steady the camera. They are generally fitted with the zoom (left) and focus (right) controls.

The tripod
A *tripod* will support the camera firmly, even on rough ground. However, the mounting cannot be moved around, and its working height is preset and cannot be adjusted on shot.

Fit a castored base (*skid*) to the tripod, and you have a *rolling tripod (tripod dolly)*. This economical general-purpose 'dolly' is easily repositioned, but smooth camera moves while on shot can be difficult.

The pedestal
The *pedestal* or '*ped*' is the workhorse of larger TV studios. Its pneumatic column on a wheeled base allows the camera height to be changed smoothly, or set anywhere within its range (e.g. 1–1.5 m (3–5 ft)), even when on shot.

Crane arms
Basically, a *camera crane* consists of a large counter-weighted *jib* or *crane arm* pivoted on the central column of a wheeled platform. This arrangement allows the camera at one end of the crane to be positioned or moved to heights from around floor level to, for example, 2 m (7 ft) or more.

A lightweight form of crane arm mounted on a pedestal or similar base is widely used today. The camera is remotely operated from controls at the rear end of the arm.

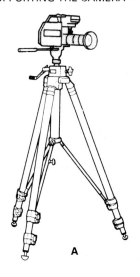

A

B

A The tripod
A stable static support; even on rough ground. Its height can be preadjusted.

B The rolling tripod
A simple yet mobile support on a castered base.

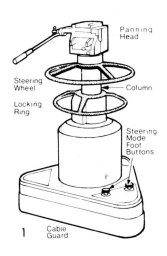

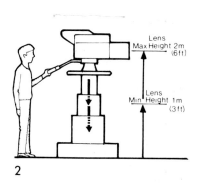

1

2

The studio pedestal
1. Turning the locking ring allows the central column to rise/fall. Maneuvered by the steering wheel, the pedestal can be moved with (a) all three tricycle wheels linked (dolly mode), or (b) one steering, two fixed (crab mode).
2. Height is readily controlled.

31

What are 'Lens Angles'?

The camera's lens shows us a wedge-shaped segment of the scene. In regular TV/video systems, its horizontal coverage is 1.33 times greater than its vertical; in other words, the screen has 4 by 3 proportions.

How much of the scene appears in the picture will depend on the angles the lens covers. If the lens covers a horizontal angle of 40°, its corresponding vertical angle will be 30°.

The actual angles will vary with the lens' *focal length* (see Glossary). A *prime lens'* angles are fixed, according to its design; but *zoom lenses* have variable focal length, and so can adjust their coverage.

Two conventions are used when planning shots. You can identify the lens either by its 'focal length', or by its horizontal 'lens angle'. Because angles are more obvious, and can be directly related to scale plans, we shall use that method here.

Zoom ratio
The horizontal coverage of a zoom lens can be changed from as little as 1.5° at the narrow angle ('telephoto') end of its range to as much as 60° at its wide angle limit.

But most zooms cover a more limited range, and a 10:1 zoom ratio (50–5°) has proved very practical for many purposes.

Image size
The lens angle determines how much of the scene is revealed from a particular camera position. A *narrow* lens angle (e.g. 10°) may pick out a single face from a row of people. Readjust it to a *wide angle* (e.g. 50°) and it may show them all. However, although we see more, sizes are proportionally reduced.

- Using a 10° lens, subjects are 5 times as large as with the 50° lens, but we see only $1/5$ as much of the scene.
- On a 5° lens, the subject will appear twice as large as on the 10° lens; 10 times that in the 50° shot.

Lens angle and perspective
Theoretically, subjects are only shown in their true proportions (*natural perspective*) if the camera's lens angle is similar to that from the viewer's eye to either side of the TV screen (e.g. 20–27°); but the eye is very tolerant. However, if you use a much narrower or wider lens angle, pictorial perspective *will* look distorted. Space, distance and depth appear exaggerated (wide angle) or compressed (narrow). With care, though, as you will see, you can turn these effects to your advantage.

WHAT ARE LENS ANGLES?

Angle of view
The TV camera lens 'sees' 4 by 3 proportions. The vertical angle of view is therefore ¾ of its horizontal angle.

Lens angles
Changes are proportional as the lens angle alters. Using a lens of three times the present angle (i.e. ⅓F), the subject now appears ⅓ of former size and ×3 of scene width is now visible. The effect is that of increasing the camera distance by three times. Changing to a narrower angle has the opposite effect.

Wide Angle Lens

The term 'wide angle' covers lens settings from, for example, 30° to 60° or more. Used carefully, the wide angle lens has great advantages . . . but there are drawbacks too!

Advantages

Zoomed out to its widest angle, the lens will take in a great deal of the scene. If you were shooting with a 'normal' lens angle, you could only get this shot by moving the camera much further away. And that's often impracticable, especially where space is restricted. It can be a great advantage to be able to show a broad overall view without your having to move your camera very far from the subject.

A wide angle lens appears to exaggerate *perspective*. Distance, space and depth seem to be emphasized. Everything looks further away than it really is. This can be a big asset in a small studio, where even a limited low-budget setting can look impressively spacious on camera.

Another plus is that *smooth camerawork* is much easier when you use a wide angle lens. Any bumps and judders when moving the camera (especially over uneven floors) are less obvious. It is a lot easier to focus too, because the *depth of field* is much greater.

Disadvantages

However, using a wide angle lens has its drawbacks. It's great to be able to show the whole of the scene in a single shot, but if you are not careful, you will see *too much* – overshooting the studio set, revealing the sound boom, lights, other cameras or bystanders too! On location, you may find that a wide angle shot includes a disproportionate amount of sky or foreground.

There are times when the way in which the wide angle lens exaggerates space can be an embarrassment; especially if a commentator refers to cramped living conditions . . . which are transformed by the wide angle lens to appear unnaturally spacious on the screen.

Another strange effect is the way in which the wide angle lens exaggerates the *speed of movements* towards or away from the camera; either as people move, or the camera dollies in and out.

With a wide angle lens, details quickly become too small and distant. But move closer to see them more clearly, and strange distortions can develop! Closeups of people on a wide angle lens are unflattering, even grotesque.

Close shots of print, music or graphs will show extreme geometrical distortion. Pan around with a lens of 50°or more, and you are likely to see verticals curving and straightening as they pass across the shot!

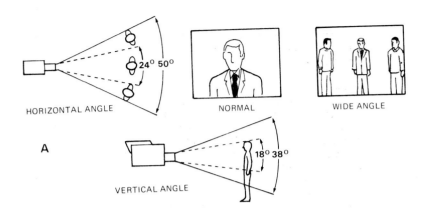

A

HORIZONTAL ANGLE   NORMAL   WIDE ANGLE

VERTICAL ANGLE

(A) Wide angle lens
For a given camera position, the wide angle lens gives an apparently more distant view, and a smaller image of the subject.

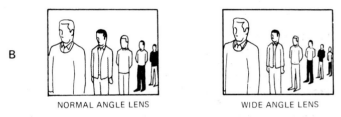

B

NORMAL ANGLE LENS   WIDE ANGLE LENS

(B) The impression of space
Whereas a normal lens angle (e.g. 24°) provides natural perspective, the wide angle lens shows apparently exaggerated perspective. (Camera distance adjusted here for same size foreground subject.)

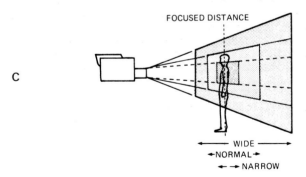

C

FOCUSED DISTANCE

WIDE
NORMAL
NARROW

(C) Depth of field
Sharpest at the focused distance, the picture remains substantially sharp over a range of distances nearer and further away. This *depth of field* becomes deeper for wider lens angles (and as focused distance increases; and for smaller lens stops).

35

Narrow Angle Lens

The term 'narrow angle' covers lens settings from, for example, 15° to 5° or less. (Generally called 'telephoto'.)

Advantages

As it fills the screen with a restricted area of the scene, the narrow angle lens gives you a 'telescopic' view of the subject. It is particularly useful when you need close shots from a distant camera, and obstacles, uneven ground or insufficient time prevent you from moving nearer with a normal lens angle.

Disadvantages

Shoot a *flat* subject, such as a painting, straight on with a narrow lens angle, and the result is identical to that with a 'normal' lens (although focusing may be more difficult).

But use a narrow angle lens to shoot three-dimensional subjects, and you will find depth that looks squashed. Distant subjects seem disproportionately nearer and larger than they really are. Things don't appear to get smaller with distance, as they should. Faces can look unpleasantly flattened and contours are reduced.

Camera handling

When you're shooting with a narrow angle lens, even slight camera shake can cause distracting picture judder. Camera movements can look uneven and jerky. The narrower the angle, the worse these effects.

On *remotes (outside broadcasts)* you often need to use very narrow lens angles (e.g. ½° to 5°) to get large enough images of distant subjects. Then you may have to *lock off* the panning head, to hold the camera firmly, rather than leave it free to tilt and pan.

Depth of field

When you 'focus' any lens, you are really adjusting the distance at which its image is *sharpest*. Nearer and further away, sharpness gradually deteriorates, until you can no longer see detail. This range of distances within which the subject appears to be acceptably sharp is called the *depth of field*. It can vary considerably, from a few centimeters to infinity, depending on the lens focal length (lens angle), the camera *distance* and the lens aperture (*f-stop*).

Whenever you *increase the lens angle* (wider angle; shorter focal length), this focused depth increases. *Reduce* the lens angle (narrower angle; longer focal length) and depth becomes much shallower; especially as the camera gets closer.

Whenever focused depth is very restricted, focusing can be extremely critical. Even slightly readjusting the focus control can throw the subject out of focus. The subject may move out of the focused region. The subject may be too large to get it all in focus!

USING NARROW ANGLE LENSES

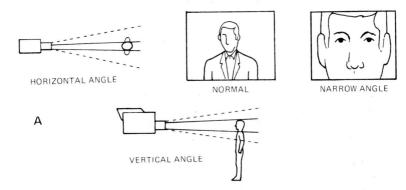

HORIZONTAL ANGLE

NORMAL

NARROW ANGLE

A

VERTICAL ANGLE

(A) Narrow angle lens
For a given camera position, the narrow angle lens gives an apparently closer view, and a larger image of the subject.

B

NORMAL ANGLE LENS

NARROW ANGLE LENS

(B) The impression of space
Whereas a normal lens angle (e.g. 24°) provides a natural perspective, the narrow angle lens shows apparently compressed perspective. (Camera distance adjusted here, for same size foreground subject.)

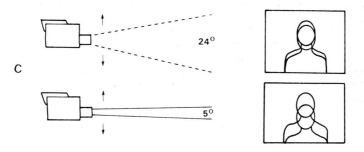

C

24°

5°

(C) Camera handling
Using a 24° lens angle a slight vertical judder of 1° (uneven floor, strong wind) produces a just acceptable jump of $1/24$ picture height. On a 5° lens, the same judder results in a considerable picture jump ($1/5$ of picture height!) With a 50° lens, it varies only $1/50$, and might be overlooked altogether.

Using the Zoom Lens

The zoom lens fitted to most TV cameras has many practical advantages, but you need to use it wisely.

Zoom lens controls
There are several different types of zoom control:
- A *manual ring* on the lens barrel.
- A *manual crank* on a panning handle, cable-connected to the lens system. The faster you turn the crank, the faster the zoom.
- A *thumb control* attached to a panning handle (usually left). This operates an electrically controlled servo system. The further you push the control, the faster the zoom action. A switch may provide different zoom rates (e.g. ×2, ×4).
- A *two-way rocker switch* is fitted to lightweight zoom lenses. This actuates a motorized zoom; often at an adjustable speed.
- A *shot box*. This is a pushbutton control box, either attached to a panning handle, or fitted into the camera head. With it, you can instantly zoom to four or five preset lens angles (adjustable), at prearranged speeds. It may also include 'wide' and 'narrow' buttons for auto-zoom, and a meter showing the *lens angle* in use.

Automatic zoom systems tend to be smoother than manual operation, and can be overridden when necessary.

Take care!
Many people change the lens angle indiscriminately, to alter the shot size. It saves moving the camera! Sometimes you may have no option, but remember, the lens angle you use can have major consequences:
- *Perspective.* If you intercut shots taken with different lens angles, your audience's impressions of size, distances and proportions will alter from shot to shot! This can upset the viewer's sense of environment or visual continuity.
- *Camera handling.* If you are following a subject on a wide lens angle, camera movements are easy, and focusing is simple. Change to a narrower lens angle, and it becomes much harder to keep the camera steady, to frame moving subjects, and to pan smoothly. And now focusing is often quite difficult, for even slight movements can necessitate refocusing.
- *Prefocusing.* Take a shot with a wide lens angle, and because there is considerable depth of field, focusing is pretty arbitrary. Zoom in to a closeup ...and you will often find that the subject is now *out of focus*! That's because the depth of field has become shallow at the narrow angle setting, and focusing is now critical. You will have to correct focus on air! The only way to avoid this embarrassment is to *prefocus the lens*; viz. zoom in beforehand, focus accurately, then zoom out for the wide shot. Now, when the time comes to zoom in, focusing will be correct.

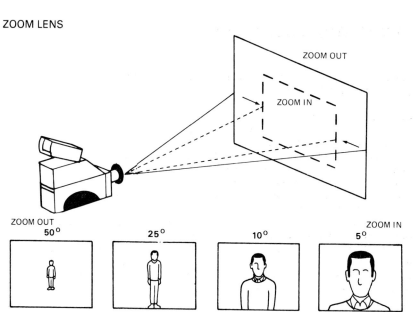

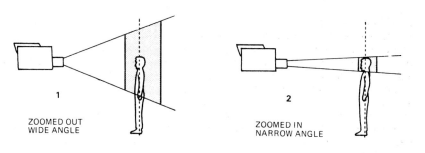

Changing the zoom lens angle

As the lens angle is reduced, and the picture *zooms in*, the image size increases and the area covered decreases proportionally.

Changing characteristics

1. At its widest angle, the zoom lens handles smoothly, and has an increased depth of field. 2. Zoomed in to its narrowest angle, these characteristics reverse, so that camera handling becomes very sensitive, and depth of field quite shallow.

Why Zoom?

If, as we have just seen, the zoom lens can be troublesome to use, why is it virtually universal? The answer is, that in the right hands it is a valuable tool. But used casually, it can lead to strange visual effects and slipshod techniques.

The effect of zooming
If you adjust the lens angle while on shot, it produces the familiar effect of 'zooming'.
- *Widening* the angle 'zooms out'.
- *Narrowing* the angle 'zooms in'.

Superficially, it seems as if the camera is moving, but look carefully. You will see that it is only magnifying and reducing *the same image*. Objects in the scene are not hidden or revealed as they are when we move around in the natural world (*parallactic movement*) with a 'normal' lens angle of around 24°.

As we saw earlier, zooming in and out on a *flat* subject is fine. In fact, it is much easier, and steadier, than moving the camera dolly to change the shot. But do the same thing when shooting solid *three-dimensional* subjects, and you will find that zooming squashes and expands space quite unnaturally.

How the zoom lens can help
If your camera is immobile (tripod mounted, on rough ground, isolated), zooming allows you to *simulate* dollying, and it provides you with a greater variety of shots. Where you are shooting a moving subject, any perspective changes will probably go unnoticed anyway.

Remember, a smooth zoom is preferable to a bumpy camera move, particularly when you need a fast 'dolly-in' or 'dolly-out' effect.

Sometimes you want to improve picture composition by tightening or loosening the shot a little. A slight change in the lens angle can be much easier and less cumbersome than moving the dolly. This technique is particularly useful when a performer fails to 'hit his marks'.

When you cut from an overall view ('wide shot') to a very localized area, the audience can become confused or disoriented. But if, instead, you *zoom in* to the detail shot, the result is an unambiguous visual bridge; without the problems of a lengthy *dolly shot (tracking shot)*.

Dramatic zooms
Zooming should always be a smooth, deliberate action. Except as an occasional visual gimmick, do avoid the nauseous results of jerky or 'in-and-out' zooming.

A fast zoom in is highly dramatic. It directs attention, increases tension, and gives powerful emphasis. But remember, a very fast zoom in (*crash zoom*) hurls detail at your audience. Distance and space squash dramatically. Conversely, a rapid zoom out creates an illusion of expansion.

You can get even stranger spatial contortions by dollying in and zooming out simultaneously!

The inaccessible subject
Where the camera cannot reach the subject, the zoom lens helps you to get a variety of shots from a fixed viewpoint.

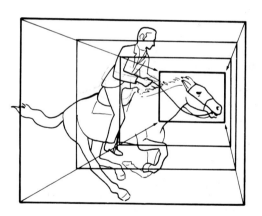

Disguising the zoom
When the subject is moving rapidly, the camera can zoom over a wide range without the resultant changes being so obvious.

41

Defining the Shot

Over the years, a universal system for classifying shots has evolved. Terms vary, but those used here are the versions you are most likely to meet.

Getting the shot
Fundamentally, when we refer to a particular type of shot, we are indicating how much of the screen is being filled by the subject; how close it appears to be. We are concerned with its *effect* – not how you actually get it. For instance, you can get a *close shot* on a close wide angle lens or a distant narrow angle lens. The perspective, distortion and camera handling will be very different, but the shot size and *depth of field* will be the same.

Changing the shot size
You can alter the size of the shot (length of shot) in several ways:
- *Changing the distance* of the subject or the camera. (Proportions and perspective remain constant.)
- *Zooming* (changing the camera angle).
- *Switching to another camera* with a different lens angle, or at a different distance.

Terms
Quite often during a production, the camera operator only needs a general indication of the shot required. When shooting people, it may be sufficient to ask for: a single shot, a two-shot, a three-shot or a group shot. The picture is then framed to include that arrangement.

Similarly, you can select:
- A *long shot* or *full shot*, for a distant view of the subject.
- A *close shot* or *tight shot* for a near view.
- A *wide shot* or *cover shot* that takes in all the action, in a broad view.

But at other times, we must be much more specific, and that is where the universal system illustrated on the opposite page is particularly useful.

Camera height
When you want to indicate the camera *height* required, the regular terms are:
- *Top shot/overhead shot (90°).*
- *High shot* (steeply inclined downwards, e.g. 40–60°).
- *Level shot* (along the eyeline or chest level, 0°).
- *Low* or *depressed* shot (upward angled, −20° to −60°).
- *Low level shot* (along the floor).

Again, it is not important *how* you get these shots; it is the effect that counts. A 'high shot', for example, could come from a camera on a crane, a camera tower or a similar vantage point. But it might simply be shooting up into a tilted mirror!

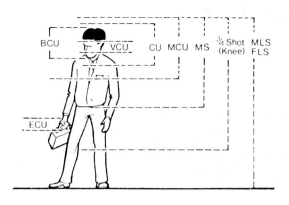

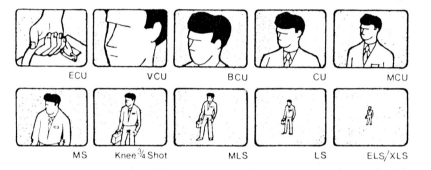

ECU	VCU	BCU	CU	MCU

MS	Knee ¾ Shot	MLS	LS	ELS/XLS

Shots are classified by the amount of a person taken in:

ECU	Extreme closeup (Detail shot) – isolated detail.
VCU	Very closeup (Face shot) – from mid-forehead to above chin.
BCU	Big closeup (tight CU, full head) – full head height nearly fills screen.
CU	Closeup – just above head to upper chest (cuts below necktie knot).
MCU	Medium closeup (bust shot, chest shot) – cuts body at lower chest (breast-pocket, armpit).
MS	Medium shot (mid-shot, close medium shot, CMS, waist shot) – cuts body just below waist.
KNEE: ¾ shot	Knee shot, three-quarter length shot – cuts just below knees.
MLS	Medium long-shot (full-length shot, FLS) – entire body plus short distance above/below.
LS	Long shot – person occupies ¾ to ⅓ screen height.
ELS	Extra long shot (XLS), extreme LS.

43

Choosing the Shot

Why do we need to bother about 'shots'? Why not present an overall view of the scene, and let the audience choose what they want to look at?

Why change the shot?
There are several very practical reasons why we need to vary the shots.
- Only closer shots will show details clearly. Wider shots are necessary to show broader action.
- A single sustained viewpoint becomes boring; especially on a small screen.
- Changes in camera viewpoint strengthen interest, and show us fresh aspects of the action and the scene.
- By changing the shot, we can redirect the audience's attention from one feature to another.
- Changes in shot allow the viewer to relate and compare.
- Intercutting can create strong dramatic effects.

Viewing conditions
How clearly your audience can see information in your pictures will depend on such factors as:
- The inherent limitations of the TV system (resolution of detail and tonal subtlety).
- The size of their TV screen, and how close they are to it. (When group viewing standard TV receivers, the effective image size can be surprisingly small.)
- The performance of their TV receiver (its design and adjustment, light falling onto the screen, etc.).
- How sharply the transmitted picture is focused.
- Contrast and color relationships in the picture.

So we see that there is a definite limit to how much detail the TV system can transmit, and how much the audience can discern. A close screen in a study carrel can include details that will be indiscernible in the home.

The picture's purpose
Whether a particular shot is effective will largely depend on its *purpose*. What is very suitable for one occasion may be disastrous for another. An atmospheric soft-focus shot will be useless if the viewer is expected to read details on a map. A wide shot will show how extensive a crowd is, but not reveal individual excitement.

Pictorial variations
The smaller the screen, the more important it is to create visual variety. While closer shots help us to concentrate on detail, longer shots reveal the surroundings, establish a mood, and allow us to follow action.

If closeups are overdone, the viewer will feel thrust at the subject, and prevented from seeing whatever else is going on. Long shots can have your audience feeling frustrated that they cannot see details in the subject, especially if these are being discussed.

The kinds of shots that *predominate* will usually depend on the type of subject you are presenting; e.g. while *dance* mainly requires longer shots, *demonstrations* make extensive use of closeups.

Viewing distance

Ideally, a photograph should be viewed so that the image subtends a similar angle to that of the original camera lens. The perspective (relative distances, sizes, depths, proportions) will then appear *natural*. Viewing distance, therefore, should really be adjusted to suit the screen size.

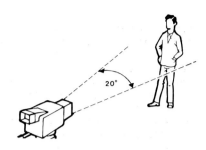

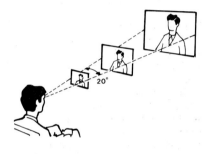

Close Shots

Close shots can show details of large objects, or provide magnified views of smaller ones. But they bring their headaches, and it is as well for the director to appreciate their limitations.

Cameraman's problems

As the camera gets closer, the available depth of field diminishes. So it may not be possible to hold the subject in sharp focus overall. Instead, you can only focus on the most important plane, leaving the rest unsharp. (You can overcome this problem by taking a longer shot, or stopping the lens down, but each remedy has its drawbacks.) To focus as sharply as possible on small items, they should be held quite still, preferably resting on a firm surface at a prearranged mark.

Cameras cannot focus on subjects closer than their *minimum focusing distance* indicates. This varies with lens design, from a few millimeters to several meters away. Even where close focusing is possible, the depth of field may be embarrassingly shallow. Lighting can be difficult, too – in getting enough light, at the right angle, without casting camera shadows onto the subject. So you often have to work further away, using a narrower lens angle.

The closer the shot, the greater the problems the cameraman has in accommodating or following action. To and fro movement requires very precise focus-following, and lateral action easily passes outside the framed area and is lost. The results can be quite frustrating! Equally annoying is the inability to discern detail, or to read information due to unsharp pictures. Although many lens systems have a *macro* position allowing sharp focusing right up to the lens surface, the basic problems still remain, and the zoom facility is inoperative.

Production problems

Although close shots reveal detail, this should be relevant, appropriate and interesting. Detail may look crude, or reveal blemishes. The audience should *want to see* this close view (or be persuaded to want it), not feel prevented from seeing other aspects that seem more interesting to them.

Close shots preclude the audience from seeing the overall view. If you use them to excess, therefore, you can prevent people from getting a clear idea of spatial relationships, or realizing where things are in the scene. They can lose a concept of proportion and scale. By moving in to very close shots, however, you can often help the viewer to appreciate craftsmanship, and subtleties that he would otherwise overlook in longer shots. Screen-filling shots of people may appear dramatic. But they can equally well emphasize complexion or dental defects.

Very close cameras can distract performers and prevent other cameras from seeing the subject. Consequently, you often find yourself taking closeups from a distance with a narrow lens angle, notwithstanding perspective and handling disadvantages.

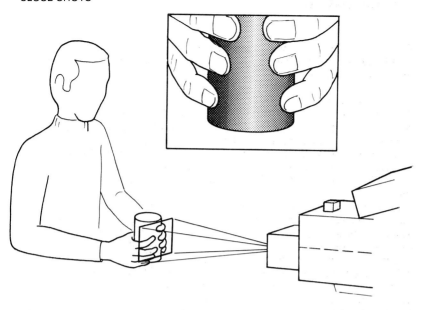

Action area
The action area in very close shots becomes extremely limited, and movements easily pass outside the shot. It is best to rest the item on a firm surface, at a marked position.

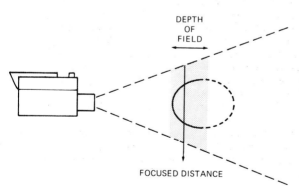

Depth of field
In close shots, the depth of field can become so restricted that only part of the subject is sharply focused, the rest becoming an indistinct blur.

Long Shots

In the studio, a *long shot* takes in an area of around 3.5 meters wide by 2.5 meters high ₁12 by 9 feet) or more.

Using long shots
A *long shot* opens up a number of productional opportunities:
- It shows the audience where the action is taking place, and helps them to get their bearings. They can see the layout and character of the surroundings, and the relative positions of people, furniture, etc.
- They can see how one part or section of a setting connects with another.
- They can see a complete group (e.g. a choir or orchestra) and locate people within that group.
- Then can follow wide movements; e.g. in a dance team.
- They can discern an overall pattern of movement or a display.
- The long shot immediately conveys a particular ambience or mood for the action. They are influenced by broad atmospheric and environmental effects that may be lost in closer shots (i.e. lighting and scenic treatment).

Some directors make it a practice to include an introductory *establishing shot* as soon as possible in each new scene, to orientate the audience.

Operational problems in continuous production
As you saw earlier, long shots can show too much!
- The wider view may overshoot the setting, which then has to be extended.
- Cameras and lights may have to be positioned further away from the action than normal, to avoid their coming into shot.
- Being further away, lighting may need to be more powerful.
- Cameras may get *lens flares* from back light.
- Cameras may have to use narrow lens angles for closer shots.

Cameras in shot
While the odd camera appearing in shot may be quite acceptable in some kinds of production, in others it would be a disaster! There are several regular ways of avoiding this happening:
- *Dolly the camera back* from close to distant viewpoints. (Time-consuming. The move may be artistically inappropriate.)
- *Zoom out* to a long shot. (But perspective changes.)
- *Cut* from a 'closeup camera' on a narrow angle lens to another beside it using a wide angle lens. (Perspective changes.)
- *Position the 'closeup camera' at an oblique angle*; even hiding it behind scenery.
- *Edit in* separately recorded closeups or *cutaways*.
- Whenever a camera dollies back or zooms out, there is always the danger that it will reveal another. It may be necessary to pull back (clear) other cameras before cutting to the wide shot, to avoid this happening.

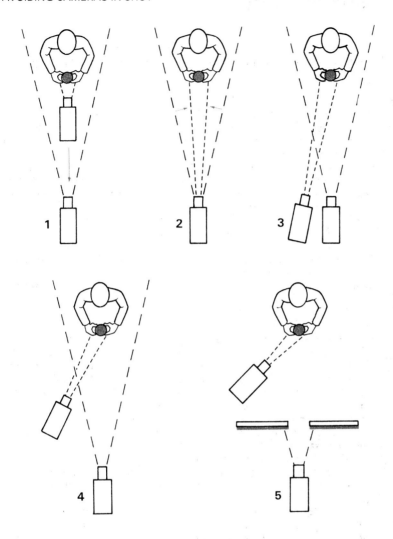

Transitions from close to distant viewpoints
To avoid another camera appearing in picture when changing from closeup to a longer shot, various methods are used: 1. Trucking (tracking) the camera out. 2. Zooming out. 3. Cutting between nearly equidistant cameras (similar viewpoints) with different lens angles. 4. Obliquely angled closeup camera (out of shot, but closer). 5. Hidden closeup camera.

Moving the Camera

How quickly you can move a camera around depends on the type and design of the mounting you are using. Even if the camera itself is lightweight, repositioning its pedestal smoothly may take some effort.

Camera moves

Although camera operators get used to coping with various operational problems, it's as well for the director to know how they can affect techniques.
- It can take time and effort to start and stop a heavy camera mounting. So smooth rapid repositioning may be impracticable.
- It is easier to push/pull a pedestal or rolling tripod in a straight line (dollying) than to *arc* round a subject in a curved track, or to move sideways (*truck/crab*).
- *Pedestals* have three tired wheels. For general movement or curved tracks one wheel is steered ('dolly' or 'tricycle' mode), while for sideways moves or confined spaces, all three wheels are linked and guided ('crab' or 'parallel' mode). It takes a moment to change between these methods of dollying.
- *Rolling tripods* have three independent castors and are generally less maneuverable. Before starting off in a new direction, a preliminary push will align the castors and avoid camera judder.
- Remember, while a *pedestal* can alter height smoothly, *rolling tripods* have prefixed heights.

Focusing

We normally maintain sharpest focus on the main subject, and *follow focus* as subject or camera moves. How critical focusing is depends on its distance, the lens angle (its depth of field), and the amount of subject detail. Close shots of finely detailed subjects shot on a narrow angle lens are most critical.

Where two subjects are at different distances, and there is insufficient depth of field to cover them both, there are several solutions:
- *Focus hard on one*, allowing the other to be *soft focus*.
- *Split focus* so that the farthest and nearest are equally focused (although neither will be really sharp).
- *Move the subjects closer together*, so that they are at similar distances.
- *Increase the depth of field* by using a smaller lens aperture (*stopping down*). This will necessitate increasing the general light levels (intensities) to avoid the shot being underexposed.

In *running shots*, where both the subject and the camera are moving, there is always the danger of losing focus. One must continually judge the available depth of field. When the camera is moving to or from a flat subject (map, chart, printed matter), the trick is to continually 'creep' focus to maintain maximum sharpness; a technique that comes with experience.

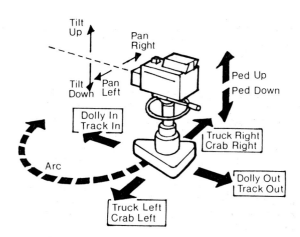

Camera moves

These terms for the various camera movements show the considerable mobility of the pedestal mounting.

51

Motivated Camera Movement

Ideally, there should be a good artistic reason behind everything you do during a production. Don't just vary the shot for the sake of visual variety or to relieve the monotony.

Motivation

Whenever you make a change of any kind that the audience does not want, or cannot understand, you have every prospect of frustrating them! If while watching someone demonstrating how to fit an accessory, you cut away to a closeup of their face, or pull out to a long shot, the viewer will resent the change.

- A camera move can arise *naturally* – zooming in as the speaker points out details.
- Or you can *deliberately create motivation*. The seated speaker gets up to fetch a book to show to camera. The move looks natural enough, but it allows the director to activate an otherwise static shot.
- You can *contrive business*, having someone sit, alter their position, turn, put down an object, as a 'reason' to change the camera viewpoint.

If there is too little movement in the subject or camera, interest falls. But excessive camera movement looks restless and fidgety. During a static scene, even a single move can become dramatic. But too many moves, and the impact of each is reduced.

Panning

Panning should be a smooth, deliberate, continuous operation. It's wise to avoid panning over a wide arc, e.g. between people some distance apart. It's far better to cut between them. Very fast pans are best reserved for startling effects (*whip*, *zip*, or *swish pan*).

Changing the viewpoint

Static, shoulder-level shots form the core of TV studio presentation. But we often want to change this viewpoint. Let us consider *why* we move.

- *Moving in to the subject* (dolly or track in, zoom in). We move in to see more detail; to concentrate attention; to exclude extraneous subjects; to identify detail; to alter scale; to follow a subject as it moves away.
- *Moving out from the subject* (dolly or track back; zoom out). We move out to accommodate wider action; to show a subject's relationship to its surroundings; to take in more subjects; to reveal the reason for a person's move; to follow someone moving away from the camera; to broaden information (from a solo singer to an entire choir); as an act of conclusion to action.
- *Moving across the scene* (truck, crab). Here we follow transverse subject movement; or survey a broad, long, spread-out subject; or a succession of subjects.
- *Moving round the subject* (arcing). Moving round a subject we can alter our scenic viewpoint; show different aspects of the subject and its surroundings; create visual variety; change the centre of interest; or recompose the shot to alter emphasis.
- *Moving to a higher viewpoint* (ped up, elevate, boom or crane up). High-angle shots can provide overall views; enable us to see over obstacles; or obtain level shots of tall or elevated subjects.
- *Lower camera viewpoints* (ped down, depress, boom or crane down). Very low positions give dramatic upward-looking shots, while low-level shots (ground shots, floor shots) give head-on views of ground level subjects.

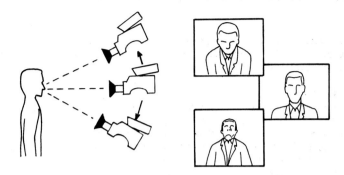

Camera height
When the camera looks down, the subject tends to appear inferior, subdued. Looking upwards, it seems dominant, powerful.

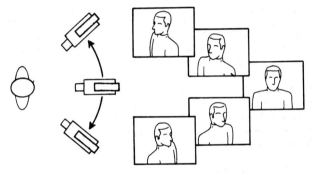

Arcing movement
As the camera moves *round*, a subject can appear to turn.

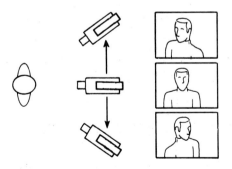

Trucking (crabbing) movement
As the camera moves *across* the scene, it obtains a more oblique view of the subject.

Composing the Picture

Pictorial composition is about creating shots that will convey a certain mood, direct the attention to particular features, and develop audience interest. The subject is complex, but let's look at some practical points to watch out for.

General approaches
- Shooting *flat subjects* straight on avoids visual distortions (squashing, keystoning).
- Three-dimensional subjects look best when slightly angled.
- Arrange subjects in related, unified groups, rather than haphazard bunches or strung-out displays.
- Shooting past things in the foreground (e.g. overhanging branches) creates an impression of depth, and emphasizes the illusion of space. But don't be tempted to continually peer through foreground foliage, fences, etc., or it will look contrived.

Arranging people
- If someone is speaking directly to the camera, a straight-on (head-on) shot has maximum impact. People speaking together are best angled, and will usually be much closer together than normal. Where people are some distance apart, shoot them from a more oblique angle to avoid a large gap between them ('cross shot').
- In cross shots, take care that people are not accidentally masked off by others in the foreground. Are you cutting off parts of heads?
- Line-ups are fine for inspections and chorus lines, but whenever possible, arrange people in groups at varying distances.
- Movements are most effective when made to and from the camera, or in a diagonal line from left to right. Moves across the screen quickly pass out of shot; particularly if they are close.
- Don't automatically place subjects in the screen center. The shot may look more balanced if they are located at a point ⅓ of the screen height and/or width ('rule of thirds').
- When someone's head is turned or in profile, place them slightly off-center in the frame ('nose room'). If they are moving, increase this offset, the faster they travel.
- Look out for things appearing to grow out of peoples' heads, to form 'haloes', 'horns', 'wings', 'hats'. Scenic lines cutting across the top of the head, chin or shoulders can create very distracting effects.

Framing
- Keep important items away from the picture edges (edge cut-off).
- Adjust the headroom between people and upper frame to suit the length of shot (greater for longer shots). Match headroom in comparable shots.
- If a shot is too 'tightly framed', the screen can seem to 'restrict' the subject. Too much space around the subject, makes it look isolated.
- Don't have subjects appearing to lean or rest on the frame.

Camera height
Use level shots wherever possible. Lower shots dramatize the subject. Higher shots reduce its strength and importance.

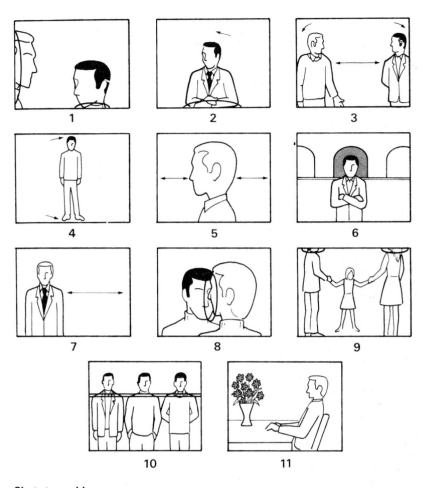

Shots to avoid

Here are various everyday compositional errors you should avoid.
1. Avoid half-heads, and body-less shots. 2. Avoid excess headroom. People
should not rest on the frame. 3. Avoid excess empty space between subjects. Do
not have subjects too near the sides of the shot. 4. This shot is too tightly framed,
with too little space at the top and bottom. 5. Always offset a profile or ¾-face
shot, to give it 'looking room'. 6. Avoid lines cutting a person, or adding spurious
extensions. 7. Centralize subjects unless they are balanced by scenic masses.
8. Avoid foreground subjects masking others. 9. Avoid decapitation. 10. Don't
align subjects across the screen (vary size, distance, and position). 11. Avoid
over-prominent set-dressing (props).

55

Clarifying the Shot

Directly a picture appears on the screen, our eyes scan over it . . . assessing, interpreting, relating it to the previous shot and accompanying sound. But what if we can't see the subject clearly, or find ourselves looking at some other feature in the picture? Our attention is diverted. Thought processes are upset. We may find it intriguing – or frustrating. We may dismiss it impatiently.

How you present subjects directly influences how successfully your ideas and intentions are conveyed to your audience.

Improving clarity
- Don't try to show too much at a time.
- Wherever possible, simplify grouping, and clear away clutter.
- Over-complicated crowded arrangements, or dual centers of attention, are usually distracting.
- Subjects stand out most clearly against plain backgrounds of contrasting tone and hue. Flat even backgrounds can look very severe, but when unevenly lit (shaded, dappling) can become extremely effective.
- Backgrounds should not predominate. Avoid bold, bright, colorful, decorated or fussy backgrounds.
- Clarity can depend on the camera's viewpoint. Even common objects can become puzzle pictures if shot from inappropriate angles.
- Try to prevent important parts of the subject becoming hidden or shadowed.

Clarify detail
Close shots
- If a shot is much too close, detail can become coarsened and over-enlarged. Very close shots of photographs can reproduce as fuzzy detailless shadows; the dot structure of newspaper illustrations, or the lines in engravings, may make enlargements indecipherable.
- Take care when showing a very localized part of a subject (e.g. small decorative detail) that your audience recognizes how this fragment relates to the complete subject.
- Include visual clues to scale whenever you show a greatly enlarged shot of a subject; e.g. a finger touching a tiny flower.
- Depth of field may be too restricted to see the entire subject clearly.
Distant shots
It's obvious that if a shot is too distant, you will not be able to discern details clearly. But it also becomes more difficult to assess shape and surface finish, as we lose texture and shading subtleties.

On the other hand, if everything in a picture is needle-sharp (deep focus), it can be difficult to see a subject, because planes at different distances merge in the flat TV picture. A subject stands out most clearly when its background is blurred (due to restricted depth of field).

Lighting techniques can improve or reduce clarity – accidentally or deliberately. Shadows and reflections may prevent our seeing surface decoration, yet help us to discern form. Frontal diffuse (*soft*) light can suppress texture and surface modeling. Hard light can overemphasize texture and form. Lit from an unsuitable angle, the shape or details of an object can be completely lost.

56

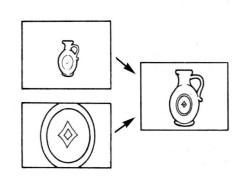

Size of shot
If the shot is too distant, details cannot be seen. Too close, and details are coarsened, and the outline lost.

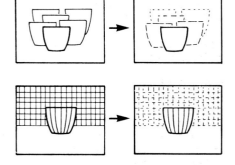

Conflicting backgrounds
Congested or over-detailed backgrounds can be suppressed by deliberately limiting the depth of field.

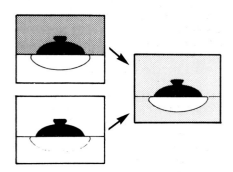

Background tones
Background tones should be arranged to suit the subject – whether by lighting adjustment, or choice of surface values.

57

The Production Switcher – Vision Mixer

Whenever you have several video sources (e.g. cameras, VTRs) you need a *production switcher/vision mixer* in order to select and blend their pictures. (The sound from these sources is routed separately, to the sound control desk.)

The basic switcher is simple enough to operate, but designs range from rudimentary, to highly sophisticated devices incorporating various video effects. There are even automated switchers that can be preprogrammed.

Where the director is preoccupied with guiding talent, camera moves, cuing, etc., and switcher operations become complex (video effects, combined shots), it is better for a separate person to concentrate on its operation – usually the *switcher/vision mixer*, or the *technical director*.

Switcher operation

● The simplest switcher has a row of *cut* buttons which enables you to switch between various video sources or 'channels' (cameras, VTRs, film, slides, etc.).

The button you select on this *program bus* or *bank* will light up when pushed, and put that source 'on air'. At the same time, its picture appears on the main color monitor (termed *line, master, transmission* or *studio out*). The output of the switcher goes to be videotaped – or transmitted if the show is live.

Interswitching produces *cuts* between picture sources.

● In most switchers, there are *two identical rows* of these cut buttons. Which row is operative, 'A-Bus' or 'B-Bus', is determined by a large communal *fader lever (bus-fader)*, that cross-fades between them. If this fader is over to 'A-Bus', 'B-Bus' is in 'standby' mode.

Punch up Cam-1 on A-Bus, and Cam-2 on B-Bus, and as you move the fader from A-Bus to B-Bus position, the screen will mix (dissolve) from Cam-1 to Cam-2's picture. Stop part way, and you have a *superimposition*.

● A further row of buttons (*Preview bus*) allows the picture from any source to be checked on a color *switchable preview monitor*. (The individual picture monitors for each source are usually monochrome.) Switching on this preview bus does not affect the studio output in any way.

These are just the basics, but even the most complex switchers are really variations on this theme.

Additional features

Larger switchers also include many refinements such as:
● *Effects buses*, or *mix banks* to control wipes, insets, etc.
● Interswitching or mixing *groups* of sources.
● *Color synthesizer* selection.
● Picture manipulation; e.g. negative/positive, inversion, mirror, ripple.
● *Title edging* ('edge generator').
● *Title insertion* ('downstream keying').
● A *chromakey (CSO)* system.
● Remote control for VTRs, film, slide sources.

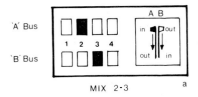

'A' Bus

'B' Bus

MIX 2-3   a

The production switcher – basic operations

MIX (DISSOLVE) between Cams 2 and 3. Select 2 on A-bus. It is now on line (on air) as the bus fader is at A. Prepare for a mix, by pressing 3 on B-bus. Push down bus fader(s) from A to B, and output mixes from Cam 2 to 3. Move fader to A-bus: output mixes back from Cam 3 to 2.

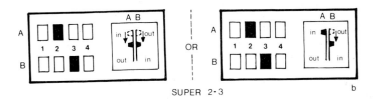

OR

SUPER 2-3   b

SUPER CAMERAS 2 and 3: Either as for a mix, stopping when superimposition strength is as required, or split faders, moving appropriate lever towards the bus to be added.

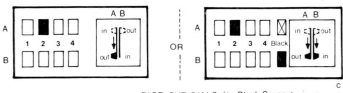

OR

FADE OUT CAM 2 (to Blank Screen)   c

FADE OUT CAM 2 (to black screen). Either split faders, pushing A-bus lever to OUT (B-bus is already faded out); or where the system would lose chroma using this method, select special *black-level* button in the other bus, and mix to black.

59

Choosing Picture Transitions

Hypothetically, you shouldn't move on to the next shot until your audience has absorbed the information, or the action is completed.
- If you don't hold a shot long enough, you may leave the viewers intrigued, puzzled, or frustrated.
- Hold it too long, and their attention wanders.
- In practice, various factors influence how long you retain any shot: how interesting it is, the action within it, how important the shot is to the program's development, the prevailing mood, and so on.

Selecting the right transition
Transitions should reflect the mood or tempo of the production. They can even alter how the audience *interprets* successive shots. Using a *cut*, when a *slow mix* would have been more appropriate, can be distracting or confusing.

The cut
The cut is dynamic. There is an immediate comparison between two shots. Action appears continuous. The *moment* you cut can be very important. Time it badly, and you can interrupt action, creating a momentary visual blip. You will generally find that a cut is best made:
- On movement within the frame; i.e. as a person gets up.
- Just as a person leaves the frame (exiting).
- Just as an action is about to begin or end.
- As the dialogue gives emphasis – not necessarily at the end of a sentence.
    Because a cut *interrupts* action, you need to be particularly careful about cutting *during* movements, or within musical phrases, or between moving and still shots.

The fade
Fading in or out of black (blank screen) generally conveys a long lapse of time. How long depends on the fade rate. *Slow fades* are gentle and peaceful. The *fade in* provides an expectant introduction. The *fade out* conveys a feeling of conclusion, or dying away.

The mix (dissolve)
The mix is comparative. It draws attention to similarities or differences between shots.
- A mix often implies a short time lapse between events.
- *Fast mixes* suggest that action in the two scenes is taking place at the same time (*parallel action*).
- *Slow mixes* provide uninterrupted picture flow – quiet, restful transitions. Often they suggest a change of time, or moving to a different location.

Wipes
Wipes are visual gimmicks. One picture breaks into another, partly or totally obliterating it. There are many wipe patterns (mainly geometrical). You can adjust their shape, speed, direction and edge sharpness to suit the moment. By wiping only part of a picture, you can *inset* a corresponding section of another shot.

PICTURE TRANSITIONS

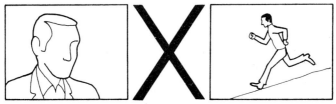

The cut
An instantaneous change from one picture source to another.

The fade-out
The gradual fade out of a picture, to a black screen. The *fade-up* is the reverse effect.

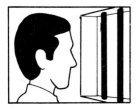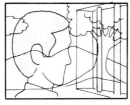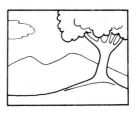

The mix
A simultaneous fade out of one picture, while fading up another. During the mix, the pictures are superimposed.

The wipe
A moving geometrical shape covers over one picture with the corresponding part of another, progressively replacing it. At a midway point, you have a split-screen effect. A wide variety of hard (sharp) or soft-edged wipe patterns is available.

61

Intercut Shots

There are occasions when one presents the audience with a shot, and invites them to look around it, choosing their own centres of interest. But more often, we want them to look at certain aspects of the scene. We want to *persuade* them to concentrate on particular features of the subjects – to watch the chemical process, not the person operating the equipment.

Guiding the audience
During most productions, the director is continually guiding the viewer's attention . . . taking their interest from one aspect of the scene to another . . . showing different features of the subject . . . introducing the viewer to new subjects.

The most obvious way of redirecting their concentration is to reframe the shot, or zoom in, or move the camera around to another viewpoint. But these methods don't allow us to make *instantaneous* changes. To do that, we need to *intercut* between shots. When a cut is made skillfully, the audience will accept it as 'naturally' as a blink, or a rapid repositioning of the eyes. Badly done, it becomes a visual jolt, that draws our attention to the transition.

Typical treatment
When people talk together (interviews, discussions), we usually *cross-cut* between them, to watch their delivery and reactions. The idea seems straightforward enough. But as you will see on the opposite page, some strange effects can develop that cause a momentary visual shock.

Above all, never cut between *nearly identical* shots of the *same* subject. Try it and see why! It is surprising how often, when left to find their own shots, a camera crew will unknowingly present a series of similar pictures. Switching between them achieves nothing but visual jumps.

You'll get a similar effect if you take a continuous shot of someone talking, then decide to omit sequences. Each editing cut causes a disturbing *jump cut* as the picture changes. Some directors ignore the disruption, or introduce a quick mix to disguise it. Even a rapid 'fadeout to black, then fade in' (*dip*) has been tried. But the best solution is to insert a *cutaway* or a *reaction* shot ('nod shot').

Shooting people
When shooting people, *reverse angle shots* intercutting frontal and rear viewpoints ('over-shoulder shots') are an effective way of showing their relative positions. But take care that you do not cause them to jump from side to side of the frame! That can happen if cameras are shooting from opposite sides of an *imaginary line* joining these subjects – *crossing the line* (page 99). Some directors ignore such niceties, and just leave the viewer to work out what is happening!

Transformations
When we cut between identical shots of different subjects, transformations take place.

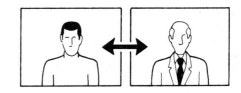

Size jumps
'Shrinkage' or 'growth' occurs on cutting to a different shot size of the subject from a similar angle.

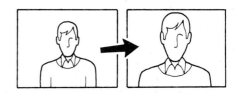

Position twists
Cutting to a similar shot of the subject, from a different angle, can create a visual 'twist'.

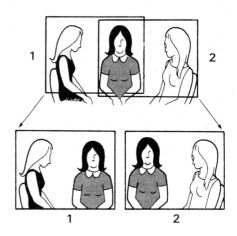

Frame jump (jump cut)
Here the frame position of the subject changes on the cut.

Choosing Microphones

Effective sound pickup involves a great deal more than just being able to *hear* what is going on!

Microphone design
There are, in fact, several *types* of microphone, including dynamic (moving coil), condenser (electrostatic), electret, ribbon. Each has its particular merits and limitations. What is more important to most users is *how they behave in use.* Do they overload easily, and distort near loud sources? Are they easily damaged? Is it the audio quality you want?

The *form* of microphone you use mainly depends on the way you are going to use it. Some are intended to be hand held, others fit certain types of mounting, or are intended for particular jobs. For example, a PZM (pressure zone microphone) uses a plate-mounted electret capsule, and is generally attached to walls or tables, for group sound pickup.

While some microphones pick up sound equally well *in all directions (omnidirectional),* others are deliberately designed to be more sensitive *in one direction (unidirectional)*; e.g. *cardioid* types. The mike can be made so *highly directional* that it virtually ignores all sounds except those in its path (*shotgun* or *rifle mike, parabolic mike*). There are also systems that are *bidirectional*; sensitive in front and behind, but 'deaf' to sources at either side (*ribbon mike*).

Some microphone systems are adjustable to whichever pickup pattern you wish to use. Combination designs are used for stereo sound pickup.

Positioning the microphone
There is an art in positioning the microphone for best results. A badly chosen microphone placed in the wrong spot can transform the quality of a musical instrument – turning a harpsichord into a 'jangle piano'. A person's voice can become unrecognizable.

Acoustics, too, directly influence the mike position. In reverberant surroundings (*live*), the reflected sounds can overwhelm the direct sound from the source, and ruin the quality. In highly absorbent surroundings (*dead*), sound pickup will be muffled and lack higher tones ('top').

It is a matter of placing the microphone so that the quality of the sound reproduced is similar to that of the source, while preserving the character of the surrounding acoustics; and that is a matter of experience.

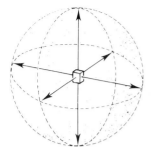 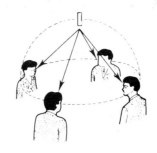

Nondirectional (omnidirectional) response
Equally sensitive in all directions.

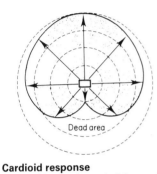 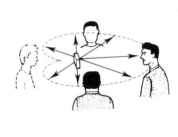

Cardioid response
A broad heart-shaped pickup pattern.

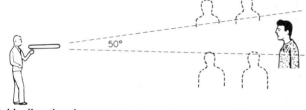

Highly directional response
Shotgun/rifle mike has a very selective coverage.

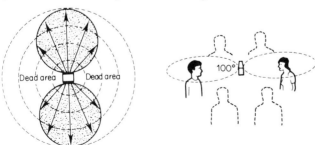

Bidirectional response
Useful for two-sided pickup, while suppressing reflected sound waves.

65

Audio Control

It is possible to treat audio control as little more than a semi-automated routine. You just clip on a mike, and rely on *automatic gain control* circuits to adjust program sound. But when you want consistent high-grade sound, or are dealing with a production of any complexity, skilled audio control is essential.

The purpose of audio control
All the production's audio sources are fed to an *audio control console (board, desk, mixer panel)*. Here the sound from microphones, disk, audio and video tape, film etc. can be selected, controlled and blended. The audio output is continually assessed on high-quality monitor loudspeakers.

The *audio quality* can be modified by emphasizing or diminishing parts of the audio spectrum; using various kinds of filter systems such as graphic equalizers/audio batons. *Reverberation* can also be added where necessary, to enhance the 'liveliness' of any source.

Audio control techniques
The *audio control engineer/sound mixer's* attention is divided between:
● Selecting each source at the right moment, and fading/switching out other sound channels where necessary.
● Adjusting the outputs of various audio sources. Checking that no source exceeds the audio system's upper limits and distorts; or becomes too quiet, and lost in the background.
● Blending the relative volumes of these selected sources, to create an appropriate *sound balance*.
● Keeping the overall strength of the final combined audio signal within the system's limits – by continually adjusting a *master fader*, while watching a volume indicator (VU meter, PPM, visual display unit).
● Following the script, and the director's intercom (talkback) information for upcoming changes, program continuity, etc.
● Checking the *technical quality* of the audio (e.g. for distortion, background noise, breaks, hum, clicks, etc.).
● Matching the *artistic quality* of the program sound with each shot, ensuring that it has appropriate *scale* (i.e. volume relative to the subject's apparent distance), the acoustics are convincing, and the overall sound balance and audio quality fit the picture.
● Scrutinize *picture monitors* (showing preview and line/transmission shots), to warn the sound crew against microphones coming into shot, boom shadows, wrong sound perspective (mike too close or too distant for the shot).
● Guide and cue various members of the sound crew who are operating booms, positioning mikes, playing audio disk and tape inserts (for sound effects, music, recorded commentary, etc.).
● Liaison with other members of the production team (director, lighting, cameras).
● Perhaps operating disk or tape equipment.

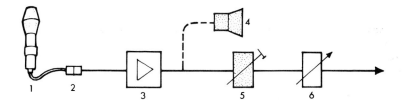

Basic audio control

Microphone (1) plugs into studio wall outlet (2) and the audio is amplified (3).
(4) A side-chain *audition/pre-hear circuit* provides check-point before further
processing. A *preset attenuator/pad* (5) adjusts channel amplification (*gain*) and a
channel fader (slide, quadrant or knob) (6) controls it overall.

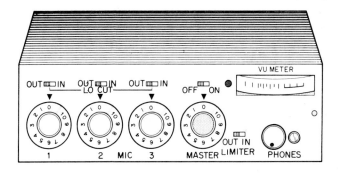

Portable audio mixer

Used in the field to mix up to three mikes; the overall output is controlled by a
master fader. A bass cut can be switched in to cut wind-rumble and improve
intelligibility. A VU meter provides a volume indicator. This mixer includes a
limiter, to prevent audio overload. A phones check-jack monitors the audio.

67

Methods of Sound Pickup

The method you use for sound pickup can directly influence the production and lighting techniques possible.

Local sound
● *Personal microphone*. A small electret clip-on mike is extensively used for speech pickup. It can be attached to the tie, lapel or shirt, or may be worn hidden beneath the clothing (with some loss of clarity). Alternatively, it may be suspended on a cord loop around the neck, as a *lavalier mike*.

Personal microphones may be used with a long trailing cable to the audio equipment, or attached to a small belt-worn radio transmitter (as a *wireless mike*), which is picked up by a nearby receiver unit.
● A *desk microphone* fitting is useful where someone is seated behind a desk or table, and an in-shot microphone support is acceptable.
● The familiar *stand mike* is most often used for stage-type performances, and to hold a detachable hand microphone for a singer. It is also used within musical groups.
● A *hand microphone (baton mike)* is a convenient and flexible method of sound pickup; but you have to rely on the person holding it to position the mike correctly! It may be cabled, or use an inbuilt wireless transmitter.
● A *slung mike (hanging mike)* suspended over the action is effective for area sound pickup (choirs, orchestras, groups).
● A *pressure zone microphone (PZM)* attached to a nearby surface is satisfactory for discussions, audience reactions, or as a table mike.

Following action
When people are moving around, you can use a personal mike or hand mike, or have them work to a series of strategically placed static microphones. But unquestionably, optimum audio quality comes only from a carefully positioned movable mike controlled by a specialist operator.
● A *shotgun* or *rifle mike* is useful for long-distance pickup; either hand held, or attached to a *fishpole* where people are fairly close but inaccessible in a crowd.
● A *small sound boom (giraffe, tripod boom)* enables you to suspend a microphone near action on its preset boom arm, and to tilt/turn the mike as necessary to follow limited movement. Because its stretch is restricted (e.g. 2.1–2.75 m, 7–9 ft), and the boom is top-heavy, tripod moves are somewhat perilous.
● The *large sound boom/perambulator boom (Fisher, Mole)* is a more elaborate, flexible device. It allows the mike to be tilted/turned on its long extensible boom arm, which can swing around freely to follow subjects from, for example, 2.5–6 m (8–20 ft) away. Although the sound boom places the mike most accurately, it needs skilled handling to avoid shadows or microphone coming into shot.

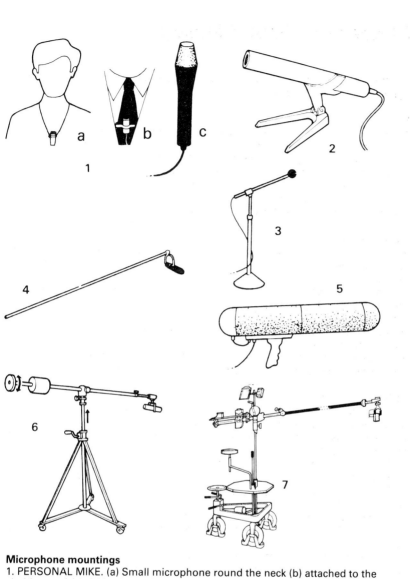

Microphone mountings

1. PERSONAL MIKE. (a) Small microphone round the neck (b) attached to the clothing, or (c) held by the performer, provides simple audio pickup. 2. DESK MIKE. A small adjustable stand supports the mike at any angle. 3. STAND MIKE. A lightweight tube or stalk, enabling the mike to be located near a singer or an instrumentalist. 4. FISHPOLE (FISHING ROD). A firm lightweight pole, holding a microphone at its far end. Invaluable for fairly close, but otherwise inaccessible, sound pickup. 5. RIFLE (SHOT GUN) MIKE. Used for pickup of distant sound over a narrow angle. Able to isolate individual sources within a group. 6. SMALL BOOM. A wheeled tripod supporting the mike at the far end of a preadjusted arm. Controls can turn and tilt the mike. 7. SOUND BOOM. The arm-length and direction can be changed quickly, and the mike direction and tilt adjusted to follow performers' movements.

69

Practical Sound Pickup

We have looked at typical methods of mounting and positioning microphones. What are their advantages and limitations in practice?

Local sound pickup
- *Personal microphone.* Simple to use, just clip the miniature mike onto the clothing. (Remember to retrieve it at the end of the session!) There are drawbacks when anyone thumps their chest (many do!), covers over the mike, or has 'noisy clothing'. Position the mike to suit the wearer's probable head position, to avoid sound coming and going as they turn the head.

   The long cable from the clip-mike to the audio equipment can be a problem. If someone moves around, they can feel tethered or get it trapped *en route*. Plugged into a pocket transmitter instead, it becomes a *wireless mike*, giving considerable freedom of movement. But this more expensive solution is susceptible to fading and interference.
- *Desk microphones* are fine, as long as people do not rustle papers or thump the table – or turn away from them.
- *Stand mikes* are liable to be moved, kicked or displaced, but are valuable for localized pickup.
- A *hand microphone (baton mike)* is excellent in the right hands, but too easily misused and badly positioned.
- A *slung mike (hanging mike)* works well for stationary sound sources, and actors who hit their floor marks.
- A *pressure zone microphone (PZM)* is easily attached to a nearby surface, but may pick up unwanted noise and reflected sounds.
- A *shotgun* or *rifle mike*, when correctly directed, is great at picking out a source, and excluding others nearby.
- A *small sound boom* is best considered as a movable suspended mike. Following action by moving its tripod is hazardous!

Using the sound boom
The large sound boom provides the most flexible method of mike placement. But it is costly, relatively bulky, and needs a skilled operator.

   The mike can be turned and tilted towards a speaker, favoring a weak voice, and reducing the prominence of a strong one. It can be positioned to avoid sound reflections from nearby walls.

   The boom can follow a moving person over an appreciable area, but it needs to be correctly located for the action. So when planning the show it's wise to ask:
- Can the boom reach the action? (Not too close or distant?)
- Is it in the best position to cover all the action?
- Is there room for the boom arm to swing, and the perambulator base to maneuver?
- Can one sound boom cover all the action? It may be necessary to track or reposition the boom, move people closer together, or pause while the boom swings to a new action area. (Supplementary mikes or a second boom needed?)

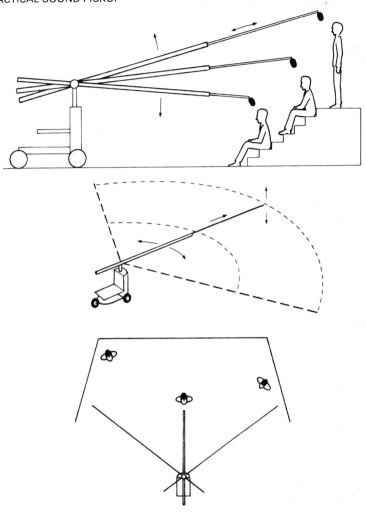

Sound boom coverage

The effective length of the boom arm can be changed, and its angle tilted, to suit variations in the subject distance and height.

The sound boom can swing over a wide arc (360° max.), and tilt vertically over some 20°, enabling it to follow sound within a considerable area.

A central boom position enables it to cover the acting area most efficiently.

71

Practical Sound Problems

Although audio problems are admittedly the sound specialist's worry, in the end it is *your* show that has these imperfections!

Ideal sound
Audio systems have their quirks. They prefer sounds that are not too *quiet*; for quiet sounds can be lost against background noises. Nor should sounds be too *loud* for the system, or they will distort, or appear out of scale. So the sound specialist (*audio control engineer, sound mixer, sound supervisor*) continually monitors audio amplification, adjusting it to keep sounds within the systems's limits (*dynamic range*), and ensure that they are in appropriate relative proportions (*sound balance*). Otherwise, a background sound might inadvertently predominate – or, alternatively, be lost altogether.

Relative volumes
Using a single microphone, problems arise when picking up loud sounds and quiet ones at the same time. Reduce the audio gain to hold the louder sound back, and the quieter may become inaudible. Two separate mikes could be the answer, but that's not always practicable.

If this dilemma arises when two people are talking together, perhaps the louder person can speak a little quieter, and/or the softer one speak rather louder. The mike might point towards (favor) the quieter voice. It is always advisable to take a *voice test (level test)* before beginning a recording, if there have been no opportunities to compare relative sound strengths during rehearsal.

A further hazard lies in the mike's *position*. If it is badly placed, the volume (level) and quality will change whenever someone turns away, and becomes 'off mike'.

Distracting sound
Background sounds can be quite distracting. The microphone seems to exaggerate many of the everyday noises around us, that we normally ignore. As well as the all too familiar accompaniment of coughs, footsteps and closing doors, there are the creaks of furniture – wicker chairs and rocking chairs are notorious! Then there is the rattling and jingling of bracelets and bangles. On location one has endless environmental noises to cope with, including telephones, passing aircraft, children at play, and the rest.

Sound and the picture
We need to take care that the volume and the quality of sound is reasonably consistent throughout a scene – particularly when shots are recorded out of sequence. Audio filters (EQ/equalization) can modify sound quality considerably, to increase realism. The same interior must not sound acoustically 'dead' in one shot, and very reverberant in the next.

Background sounds should seem continuous; e.g. the sounds of rain, traffic, birdsong, music. Such sounds are regularly added *afterwards* during post-production editing, perhaps with *sound overlays* bridging from one scene to the next.

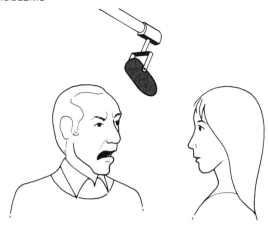

Uneven voice levels
Where quiet voices and loud voices are speaking at the same time the audio system is left at a disadvantage.

Background noise
Where there is a high level of background noise, speech may become inaudible.

Scenery

Most settings (sets) are built up from a series of 'stock' scenic pieces. These prefabricated units are selected, decorated and arranged to create a wide range of environments. They can be augmented by various additional features such as drapes, scenic cloths (*backdrops*), decorative screens and panels, and modular units.

The function of scenery
Effective scenic design makes a major contribution to the success of any production; creating a sense of occasion, giving it authority.

Scenic design can take many forms. It can provide neutral surroundings for the action. Its emphasis can be decorative or symbolic. Out of unpromising materials it can conjure 'reality'. Scenic treatment can range in complexity from a plain *cyclorama* to a painstaking replica.

Scenic design includes all the subtleties of *set dressing* – selection/arranging furnishings, ornamentation, providing various *properties*. It may even involve organizing the graphics and titling.

Devising scenic treatment
Ideas for the scenic treatment may come from the script, from the director, or from the set designer.
- Sometimes the director requires a particular arrangement or layout to fit the way he/she visualizes the production. The designer then interprets and develops this staging format into a practical treatment.
- More often, after reading the script and preliminary talks with the director, the set designer originates the staging arrangements, and submits this rough plan (perhaps with sketches). The director then works out production treatment, bearing in mind any special shot opportunities the designer has provided.

Typical design considerations
The camera shows the outward features of the set designer's art, but behind this facade lies a great deal of know-how and painstaking organization. As well as being appropriate to the subject and the program's purpose, scenic treatment has to satisfy many practical requirements:
- The allocated budget. With ingenuity, impressive effects can be created with modest means.
- The scenery must be sufficiently ruggedly built, yet allow easy handling, transportation and storage.
- Scenery must be related to the studio's dimensions and facilities. It's of little use if it will not go through the studio access doors!
- Its design must take the particular needs of the *action* into account (e.g. allowing Romeo to climb up to Juliet's balcony).
- Layout and design must provide the director with maximum shot opportunities, and anticipate specific shots.
- There must be sufficient operational space for cameras, sound booms etc. to be moved around, in front of and within settings.
- Settings must be designed to allow appropriate lighting and sound treatment.
- Various safety aspects need to be considered: structural safety, fire, water leakage, hazards to performers, etc.

74

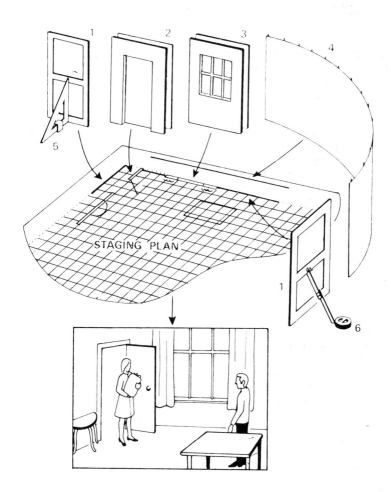

Basic staging units

The TV setting is structured from a series of prefabricated units that can be redecorated and conjoined to build a wide variety of environments.

1. Flat. 2. Door flat. 3. Window flat. 4. Cyclorama. 5. Jack (hinged scenic support). 6. Stage brace (extensible, bottom-weighted support).

The Aims of Lighting

Lighting is certainly elusive! If you walk round a *studio setting*, the skills that have gone into its creation are obvious. But you can only judge the effectiveness of *lighting treatment* when you see the specific shots for which it was designed, *on the screen*!

Technically speaking
The intensities, contrasts and directions of the lighting must suit the electronic camera's characteristics, and be appropriate for each camera angle. The light's *color temperature*, too, must be consistent throughout, or color quality will vary.

However ambitious the lighting design, it must always work within the various practical limitations of power, equipment availability, time, labor, etc.

Artistically speaking
You can use light to emphasize or suppress shape and texture; to create illusions of space and distance. Through light and shade, you can build up an atmospheric effect or set a mood. You can draw attention to specific areas, making some prominent while others recede. Through the way you light a subject, you can alter its entire appearance, giving harsh, unsympathetic lighting treatment, or enhancing attractive effects at the touch of a button.

Basic lighting approaches
Certain fundamentals underlie all lighting techniques:
● The general character of light varies from *hard light* that casts strong shadows and reveals texture and modeling, to *soft light* that is diffused, producing shadowless illumination, and generally suppressing texture and modeling. Effective lighting is a blend of both kinds.
● The directions of light sources you use, their relative intensities (*balance*), and the character of their illumination (*hard/soft*), will determine what the subject and the scene look like.
● Each subject should have a *key light*; the main luminant that creates its modeling, reveals its shape and texture, and establishes the light direction.
● A *fill light (filler)* is added opposite the key, to provide diffused light which illuminates shadows and reduces contrast.
● A *back light* behind the subject outlines it with light, helping to add depth and solidity.
● A basic lighting setup uses three light sources (key – fill – back) arranged in a triangular layout.
● In addition to subject lighting, *set lights* are used selectively, to reveal and model the setting, and create an appropriate atmospheric illusion.

The effect of lighting changes with the light's direction relative to a camera's viewpoint, and with the position of the subject. So lighting treatment is designed to suit subject movement and camera angles. It must also allow for camera and sound boom maneuvers, and avoid spurious camera or boom shadows. Clearly, successful lighting can only come from imaginative, anticipatory and systematic planning.

76

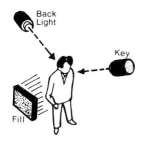

1

Three-point lighting
The main *key light*, the diffused *fill light* (that illuminates and softens the shadows), and the *back light* that outlines the subject, form the basis of most lighting treatment.

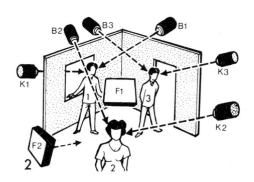

Complex lighting setups
Even a complicated lighting setup can be analyzed into its component parts. Here the respective lights for each person are K – key, F – fill, B – back. Additional lamps may light the background.

Lighting Problems

Effective television production is based on *teamwork*. One person's dilemma can often only be solved by another's action.

Lighting and sound
Sound booms cast shadows. The trick is to angle the key light so that these shadows are thrown out of shot, and not onto the talent or nearby scenery. When shadows *do* appear in shot, there are several solutions:
- Position the mike further away from the speaker.
- Reframe the shot so that the shadow is not seen.
- Take a closer shot.
- Hide the shadow in a dark area of the background.
- Reposition the key light or the talent.
- Use a *soft* (diffused) key light.

Shadows
Shadows are the essence of dynamic lighting. But when they fall in the wrong place, they can be extremely distracting.
- A heavy shadow beside a person standing near a wall. (Move them further from it, and angle the key.)
- A person's shadow falls onto his neighbor's face. (A slight head tilt or repositioning may cure the problem.)
- Someone's shadow falls onto a map they are discussing. (Key from another direction; readjust their position.)
- The camera's shadow falls onto the subject. (Raise the key; lower the camera; take camera further away.)

Subject position
It's best to avoid placing people close to walls, right in the corner of a room, tucked behind a pillar, or underneath an overhanging feature (e.g. ceiling, arch, chandelier). These situations restrict lighting angles, and shadows may be difficult to avoid.

Overbright surfaces
Excessively bright surfaces *burn out* as blank detailless areas in the picture, whether they are too light in tone, too shiny, or overlit. Sometimes it is possible to adjust the lighting, but you may need to:
- Substitute the article (e.g. use darker drapes instead).
- Darken with water-soluble spray, or dull with wax spray.
- Change the subject's position (e.g. slightly angle or move it).
- Cover over the bright area (e.g. hide a bad reflection).
- Remove the object altogether.

Precision lighting
Generally speaking, most lighting falls into two categories: *general lighting*, where we provide broad area treatment, which is modified where necessary to suit shots during rehearsal; and *specific lighting*, carefully angled and adjusted to suit particular planned shots.

The effect of light changes if you reposition or re-angle the subject or the camera. What was previously a frontal key can now become a side or back light! So major deviations from the originally planned shooting angles can produce unpredictable results. Revising the lighting treatment to compensate may upset earlier shots.

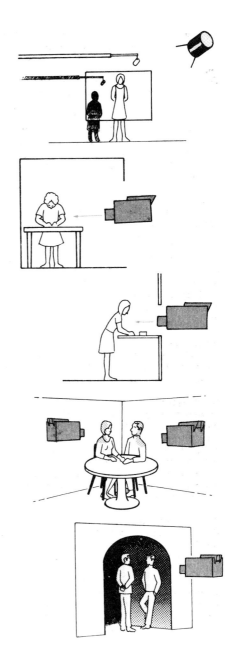

Boom shadows
Boom shadows will usually distract; particularly if they are moving or unsteady.

Subject positions
It is well to avoid positioning people beneath low ceilings.

Placed close to a camera trap, the camera can see, but lighting is difficult.

When people sit close to walls, or in the corners of rooms, close-shooting cameras may shadow them.

Lighting underneath arches and overhangs is often poor.

79

The Aims of Makeup

Television makeup treatment takes three broad forms:
- 'Straight makeup' – general improvement, without altering the basic appearance.
- 'Corrective makeup' – compensatory makeup, enhancing the features, and suppressing/disguising facial defects.
- 'Character makeup' – changing the appearance to conform with a particular type or character.

The value of makeup
Sometimes a person's natural complexion, or everyday makeup, looks fine on camera, and no additional treatment is needed, apart from tidying the hair, and a few touches to neaten their appearance – treating perspiration around temples and brow, or a distracting shine on the nose, forehead or bald head.

A *straight makeup* aims to improve the talent's overall appearance, while altering it as little as possible. Treatment can help, for instance, to even out a blotchy complexion, reduce bags under the eyes, improve skin tones, or subdue a dark beard line.

Makeup can give vitality and form to a face that the camera shows as rather lacking definition. It can emphasize the more attractive points, while reducing less flattering features. Makeup can strengthen and enhance in many ways; e.g. by making the hairline more definite; or strengthening the jaw line, chin or nose by subtle shading to improve their shape.

The magic of makeup
All makeup relies on a series of quite simple principles; but the subtlety with which they are applied is the secret of the art.
- Lighter tones advance, and make an area look more prominent, and larger.
- Darker tones recede, and make an area look less prominent, and smaller.
- Progressive shading can alter the apparent contours of a surface; e.g. so that cheeks appear to recede.
- Makeup can obliterate an existing feature, and by redrawing, shading or highlighting, create another – e.g. eyebrows.
- Makeup can emphasize a feature – e.g. making eyes more prominent.
- Existing features can be physically readjusted – e.g. taping back ears.
- Skin can be stretched, contracted, built up – e.g. simulating wounds, scars.
- Existing features can be augmented – e.g. morticians' wax and nose plugs to change nose shape.
- Existing features can be hidden – e.g. 'bald head' cap worn over hair to create a 'shaven head' look.

General practice
Where makeup cannot be carried out beforehand, the makeup artist has to rely on experience to select the most suitable treatment. Wherever possible, though, it is better for the talent to be made up before camera rehearsal. The makeup artist then carefully checks rehearsal shots, and notes whether any changes are needed. Before recording, this treatment is refurbished ('freshened up') as necessary.

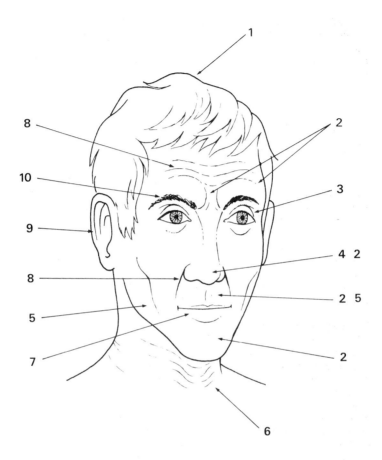

Basic makeup improvements
Makeup can help to improve or hide various visual shortcomings:
1 Shiny bald head. Untidy hair. Scalp shows through thin hair. Hair too light, or dark and dense to show well on camera.
2 Perspiration shine.
3 Deep eye sockets. Eyes too prominent. Eyes lack definition.
4 Shiny nose. Nose coloration prominent.
5 Beard-line prominent despite shaving.
6 Neck scrawny.
7 Normal lipstick too light or dark on camera. Lips need definition or shaping.
8 Age-lines, wrinkles, over-prominent.
9 Ears too light; different color from adjacent skin. Too prominent.
10 Eyebrows untidy; over-prominent; barely discernible.

Clothes on TV

For many types of show, talent wear their own clothing. They feel at ease in it, and have probably chosen it with thought. So one needs to be sensitive to their feelings and taste, before suggesting that any item is unsuitable for the camera. That is particularly true when you want them to wear an item from wardrobe stock instead (e.g. a tinted shirt, or a different necktie). Experienced performers often bring along alternative items of clothing for selection on camera.

Problem clothing
Line
Loose-fitting floppy clothing produces an unflattering shapeless, baggy look.
Color
• Muted plain colors are generally very successful.
• Bright, bold saturated colors are best avoided. Strong hues look dynamic in long shots, but appear overwhelming and somewhat crude in closer shots. Their color can reflect onto the face and neck.
• Some color mixtures can appear to change on switching between cameras (e.g. mauves, purples).
• When using *chroma-key* any blue in the clothing can produce bizarre breakthrough effects.
• Clothing tones and colors should preferably contrast with their background.
• Avoid high tonal contrasts. Light-toned materials easily 'burn out'/'block off' on screen. Conversely, very dark materials reproduce as a black mass.
• While someone is wearing a coat/jacket, the limited amount of white shirt showing may be quite acceptable. But when the jacket is removed, the larger area revealed simply overexposes to blank white.
• Dark clothing makes a light complexion look lighter. In light clothing, skin tones appear darker.
• Very low necklines can result in a topless look in close shots.
• Stiff clothing materials can cause crackles and rustles when a personal microphone is worn.
Surface finish
• Shiny, lustrous clothing catches the light, and reproduces with large burned-out areas of plain white. Even quite dark materials with a gloss finish can prove unsatisfactory for this reason. Highly reflective fabrics, such as starched shirts and satins, invariably block off.
• Velvet and velours are so light absorbent that modeling is poor.
Detail
• Strongly contrasted or elaborate patterns can be overwhelming, especially in closer shots.
• Avoid close herringbone or checkered patterns, or close fine stripes. They can produce a vibrating 'moiré' effect. Close patterns can look very distracting when sharply focused. When defocused or in longer shots, they degrade to an overall tone.
• Jewelry and decorative accessories easily look excessive on the small screen. They can produce distracting flashes, cast shadows onto the face, or make a noise. Reflective jewelry worn around the neck can reflect bright spots of light under the chin.

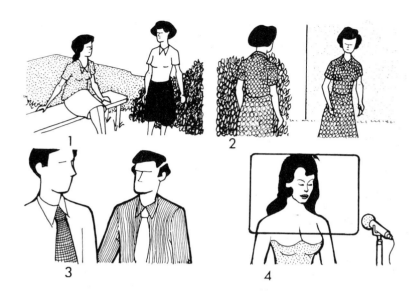

Costume problems
1. Avoid costume tones merging with the background. 2. Beware detailed or fussy patterns in both costume and background. 3. Close stripes and checks in costume flicker (strobe) at certain distances. 4. Low necklines appear topless in close shots.

The Need for Production Techniques

Although it's hard to appreciate at times, the screened image is a totally artificial, stylized representation of the real world!

Whenever we frame a segment of the scene with the camera lens, we are detaching it from reality. The audience sees only what the director chooses. They have little idea what is happening around.

The lens conveys *impressions* of scale, distance and proportion that are often quite false. A tiny object can dominate the screen, while a gigantic subject passes unnoticed. But *we* accept the result as reality.

Why have 'techniques'?

There are various reasons for today's production techniques:

• The TV screen's size limits the amount of information that we can discern. If we want the audience to see a broader view of the scene, to locate themselves perhaps, a *long shot* is needed. Where we are concerned with interactions between people, a *medium shot* may be necessary. To see specific details, only a *closeup* will suffice. And so we continually alter the shot's size and direction, to present these various aspects of the subject and the scene.

• As our center of interest moves, the shot needs to alter – e.g. from a wide shot as a person speaks to us, to a closeup showing us the coin they are holding. If we cannot see properly, we become frustrated. If a shot is held for too long, our interest falls.

• In most programs, the director is presenting a sequence of points: directing the audience's attention to particular aspects of the action or the scene, showing, for instance, how an action (throwing a ball) has a particular result (it breaks a window). Whether we *see* this result, *hear* it, or both, will depend on the kind of impact the director wants to make on the audience.

• Effective directing techniques encourage audience reaction. They do not merely present images for them to watch. They *arouse interest, persuade, intrigue* . . . They encourage the audience to *respond*.

• Because subjects are presented *within a frame*, we get subjective impressions of 'balance', 'grouping', 'unity' and 'pattern' that *we never experience in everyday life*. (One takes advantage of these phenomena when composing a shot.)

• Some production techniques are imitations of our own *natural* responses (e.g. moving the camera in for a closer view). Others are quite *stylized conventions* (e.g. wipes, inserts, mixes). Some visual devices are introduced primarily to overcome the mechanics of production (e.g. 'cutaways' when editing an overlong speech).

• Many production techniques have now become part of the understood grammar of the medium. If we use them carelessly, this can destroy the empathy of communication with our audience.

Guided selection

Faced with a crowded, active scene the eye would wander at random if offered free selection. Guided selection concentrates on local detail or action. In a wide angle shot, details are so small that they lose individual impact. Spurious factors distract the attention.

Production Treatment

Effective production techniques do not necessarily involve extensive facilities. A slow, continuous panning shot over the scene of desolation following an earthquake can convey its extent, and the sheer brooding despair, far more significantly than an elaborate intercut montage.

Back to basics
You can think of each shot as an *'information package'*. Ideally, a series of shots within any *sequence* or *scene* should form a *continuous thought process* in an argument or a story line. Each shot in a sequence should normally develop logically from the last . . . unless you are aiming at a sudden dramatic or comic impact. If your audience cannot follow the linkage between shots, they are likely to be distracted, as they try to work out what is happening.

Formality and informality
By careful composition, you can direct and hold the viewer's attention. But if the picture appears too deliberately 'arranged', it can look unnatural and mannered.

Some directors have tried to create an 'informal' style, by using a hand-held camera 'subjectively'. Where the 'formal' method would cut to someone who interrupts during a discussion, the 'informal' method would pan around the scene and zoom in on them, even if focus has to be corrected and the shot wavers. When you are working with a single camera, this might be your only option, but it is a method to be used with care. It has been introduced into documentaries, where, for example, to create an exciting subjective effect when exploring a battlefield, the hand-held camera has jumped, run and climbed, to the sound of fighting. Whether this added to the exposition, or was simply a visual gimmick, brings us to the borders of taste and judgment.

The right approach
There is no 'correct' way to present a subject; but there are certainly many *wrong ones!* Inappropriate techniques can confuse, mislead, or simply be ineffectual. Successful methods can produce such a smooth flow of events that the audience is completely unaware of the mechanics of the production. If the viewer thinks, 'Oh boy! What a great zoom!', then he has been affected more by the techniques than the subject . . . yet it's the *subject* that matters. Directors are sometimes carried away with their own 'cleverness', for instance by intercutting a sequence of shots to the beat of fast music. The result may be fascinating, but it does nothing to convey *ideas*, and it will probably frustrate the viewer with tantalizing glimpses.

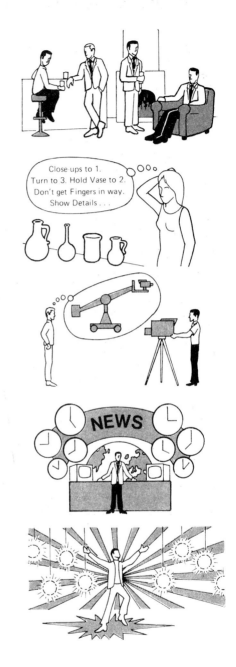

Established convention
Would a quiz game look more interesting shot in everyday surroundings?

Instructing talent
Do not preoccupy talent by overloading them with excess instructions.

Know your facilities
Always plan your show with the *available* facilities in mind.

Over-elaborate staging
The setting should be appropriate in content and style to the purpose of the production.

Visual spectacle
Over-ornamentation can pall, and visual novelties need careful handling.

87

Styles and Formats

In some types of production, scenery, lighting and camerawork make major contributions to the show's success. In others, they play an unobtrusive supporting role. The balance can be a fine one.

Present a pianist in a fully lit area against a plain background, and the visual appeal on camera will be pretty low. But a superficial 'imaginative' presentation could be equally disastrous, with cameras continually moving around, lighting changing, superimpositions blending different viewpoints . . . One must take care that production treatment does not overwhelm performance.

Presentational emphasis

Let's look at ways in which the emphasis can vary in typical productions:

- *Demonstrations* of all kinds, from cookery to auto-repairs, have common features. They use carefully controlled closeups, concentrate on detail, show the relationships between parts, compare differences in appearance. Speeded up or slowed down action may help to show developments more clearly.
- *Spectacle* can describe most large-area events from sports to orchestral concerts. These programs present their own particular quandary. When you show long shots of the overall activities, you may be missing interesting detail amongst individual performers. While you are showing closeups, important general action may be lost. Switch too early, and action hasn't started. A moment too late, and it's all over!
- *Talk shows* include interviews, discussions, and many game shows. Although shots are relatively static, the interplay between participants, and captured reaction shots, enliven the show's spontaneous visual appeal.
- *Drama presentations*, which range from soap operas to Shakespeare, can explore all the sophistications of TV grammar − the subtle influences of camerawork, editing, lighting and sound. But one needs to avoid the temptation to overdramatize, and treat 'ham' as 'Hamlet'.
- *Composite presentations* such as news programs (current affairs) and magazine programs intersperse studio material (e.g. a commentator or experts) with inserts from videotape, film, graphics, slides, etc. They often rely on interlinking contributors from many different locations. In this kind of production, the director is preoccupied with precise cuing, accurate timings, and smooth continuity. So the actual presentation format is usually quite straightforward.
- *Compilation programs* generally provide a summary or a survey of a subject. They are usually built up from a series of excerpts from library/stock sources (e.g. newsreels) which are blended together by an in-shot or voiceover commentator.
- *Non-visual subjects (see 'Visual padding')* are indeed a challenge to the director, who has to provide a flow of pictures which are apposite, neither too banal nor overfamiliar, neither too arresting nor too obscure. In most instances, the director resorts to brief library clips, and abstract effects.

Formal and dull
The symmetrical, balanced composition is dull and monotonous to the eye.

Posed shots
Composition has been carefully arranged here for dramatic effect. It could be mannered and too obviously arranged, or a powerful, naturally-evolved composition for the subject in hand.

Arranged display
The pattern the dancers make adds to the visual appeal of the presentation.

Contrived pattern
The seated speakers, sitting in an identical pattern, look inappropriately arranged. The effect is awkward and strange.

Basic Productional Methods

The settings are lit; talent, cameras and sound are in place . . . Now there are several ways in which you can organize the rehearsal/recording process.

'Live' production
To present a complex *live transmission* that is free from mishaps requires careful organization, clear-headed direction, and closely coordinated skilled teamwork. Any problems that arise while on air have either to be covered up in some way or simply accepted.

'Live on tape'
The simplest method of using videotape is to camera-rehearse the entire show. If anything does not work out, either rehearsal is stopped to correct the error, or notes are given at the end of rehearsal. There may then be a final *dress rehearsal.* A straight-through performance is then recorded as if it were 'live', using the production switcher to intercut between picture sources. The resulting *live-on-tape* version requires no further editing, and is ready for transmission.

A technical advantage of this method is that the entire show is an original *first generation* recording, without the deterioration in picture quality that subsequent editing can introduce.

Basic retakes
Here, after full rehearsal, the production is recorded continuously as before. However, if there are errors of any kind (fluffed lines, wrong cuts, sound faults, etc.), performance stops, and the bad section is repeated. It may be recorded over the original take (*assemble editing*) or separately, to be *inserted* afterwards in its place.

Discontinuous recording
In this method, individual shots/sections are rehearsed then recorded, in any convenient order. Separate corrective retakes are recorded before going on to the next sequence. It is essential to keep an accurate log of the shots! This 'rehearse-record' process is very time-consuming, and has various disadvantages (e.g. continuity errors, insufficient time to remedy problems in the setting, lighting, costume, etc.).

Isolated camera (ISO)
Here in a 'live' or 'live-on-tape' production, the cameras' outputs are interswitched at the production switcher as usual, and recorded by the main VTR. However, one selected camera's pictures are *also* continuously recorded on a *separate* VTR. The ISO camera usually concentrates on taking *cover shots, replay inserts, or standby shots*, which can be replayed or edited into the program, to avoid important action being missed, or to fill lulls in the action.

Dedicated VTRs

In this multi-camera approach, each camera's entire output is recorded on its separate VTR. Their videotapes are used during post-production editing, to form a composite master tape.

Single camera recording

A single camera is used throughout a 'rehearse-record' session, its output being recorded on board (as in a camcorder) or on a separate VCR. Tapes are subsequently edited to form a composite master. (It is preferable not to 'edit in camera' by pausing tape between shots, or wiping/inserting during shooting.)

The advantages of videotaping

• You can check each section you record, before going on to the next.

• It gives an opportunity to improve or correct any performance, and eliminate operational errors (e.g. cameras in shot). *Retakes* may be edited in, during or after the recording session.

• You can record sequences in any convenient order; to simplify staging, camera operations, makeup or costume changes, etc.

• You can improve the presentation (e.g. tighten the pace, omit pauses).

• You can effectively increase your facilities; e.g. reshoot a scene from different camera positions, to produce a 'multi-viewpoint' presentation when these shots are all edited together.

• Changes can be made during recording pauses; e.g. repairing makeup, altering scenery and lighting.

• Many refinements can be introduced during post-production editing, e.g. replacing or inserting new material, adjusting overall or sectional durations by adding or cutting.

• The actual shooting session can be shortened and simplified by adding music, video effects, commentary, subtitles, etc., during a later editing session.

• You can also alter or manipulate the sound and pictures afterwards (e.g. build up multi-image video effects); a process that would have used valuable studio time during the original taping session.

• The production can be recorded in duplicate to provide a *protection copy/backing copy*.

• Program scheduling is easier with videotape recordings than live transmissions. They are reliable packaged products of known duration.

Single Camera Production

Some directors prefer to work with a single camera, for they feel more directly involved in the action, and better able to make on-the-spot decisions, than when directing from the production control room.

Intermittent shooting

This is the way most single camera productions are shot. They are videotaped in a series of brief camera setups, using *rehearse-record* techniques. Action is repeated wherever necessary, to provide visual continuity between different viewpoints. The takes are later sorted and edited together.

Continuous shooting

But this is not the only method you can adopt. Instead you can shoot *continuously*; either 'live' or 'live on tape'.

How do you shoot extended action lasting several minutes or more with a single camera?

Of course, you could simply move around from one viewpoint to the next, zooming in and out to adjust the shot size. But although this 'roving camera' approach is acceptable in a news item, for most other productions the audience would soon become over-aware of the continually moving camera, particularly if the subject itself does not move.

To disguise camera mechanics, have the performer move around, and make any changes *during their movements*. For example, if you want to transfer attention from one area to another, have the camera move with a demonstrator. It pans as he goes to the next item. The camera tilts (or depresses) as he looks down at it. We zoom in as he points out a feature. All the camerawork seems 'natural' and unobtrusive.

Shooting static subjects

• A shot where subject and camera are quite still will normally only sustain attention for half a minute or less – depending on how interesting the viewer finds it.

• Wherever possible avoid panning over a series of subjects lined up *across the shot*. It's a visual bore! It's better if you place subjects at different distances from the camera. Then the shot size and composition will change as the camera concentrates on one after the other, by panning or zooming.

• To create visual variety, you can place a static subject such as a piece of sculpture, a vase or a floral display on a turntable, which rotates to show different features. The result is similar to that of a camera arcing round it.

• Occasionally, you can prolong a static shot by slowly pulling focus from items in the foreground to others in the background.

• You can create an illusion of animation by introducing lighting changes; for example, starting with the subject in silhouette, lighting progressively reveals features.

• If you have a second video source, such as a videotape deck, graphics camera or film channel, you can switch to this while repositioning the camera or altering the shot.

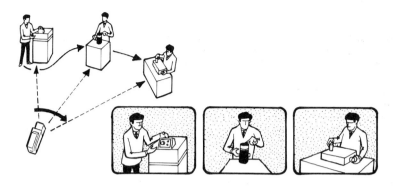

Subject movement and the single camera – equidistant positions
Items can be arranged equidistant from the camera, to provide a series of similar shots as the talent moves around

Subject movement and the single camera – movement in depth
Where subjects of various sizes are involved, the largest can be located furthest away, the smallest closest to the camera.

93

Multi-camera Production

When shooting continuous action with a *single camera*, there will be times when you have to dolly or zoom, just in order to make room for another person in the frame, or to recompose the shot when they exit. This need never happen in multi-camera production.

Why have a second camera?
There are great advantages in having a second (or third) camera:
- A single camera has difficulty in covering continous action over a wide area; especially when one event begins immediately after another, or when events overlap. Multi-cameras can be prepared for widespread action.
- You can redirect the audience's attention in an instant, by switching to a second camera – to introduce fresh information, to alter emphasis, to point out new detail, to compare, or simply for visual variety.
- When shooting live, you can change the shot size or intercut camera viewpoints without missing a moment of the action.
- Having two or more camera viewpoints can ensure that one always has a clear view of the action.
- A multi-camera setup avoids the need to interrupt and repeat action just in order to move your camera to a new setup. Consequently, it avoids continuity problems.
- When you videotape a multi-camera production, all editing can be carried out with the *production switcher*. This saves a great deal of time, and you can have a *complete* production package by the end of the session.
- You can *combine* two cameras' pictures in various ways:
  - To superimpose subtitles.
  - To introduce extra information (e.g. a background map behind the action shows its location).
  - To insert a small detail shot within the main shot.
  - To create a special effect (wipe, split screen).
- You can have one camera taking wider shots, while the other(s) concentrates on closeups of the action, reaction shots, and cutaways.
- While one camera shows a lecturer, the other can provide intercut detail shots of what is being discussed (e.g. maps, models, artifacts).
- Where you are using *optical effects* (e.g. a multi-image lens), it can be fitted to one camera, while another provides normal pictures.

Are there disadvantages?
Of course, multi-camera production can have its drawbacks too:
- To use cameras efficiently, you need to plan their shots and moves beforehand, especially if the action is complicated, and to convey your ideas in advance to the camera operators (script, camera card).
- Intercom instructions to cameras and switcher operator need to be clear and anticipatory.
- Switcher operations must be accurate, especially when it is not possible to correct errors.
- You must avoid cameras getting into each others' shots.

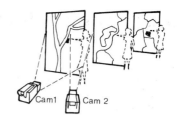

Two-camera treatment
Here shots are divided between two cameras. Cam 1 concentrates on long shots. Cam 2 takes closeups of maps and speaker.

Cam 1   Cam 2

Maximum use of cameras

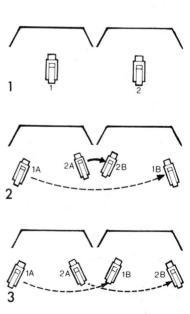

1 One camera to each set is unnecessarily restrictive.

2 Near the end of a two-camera scene. Cam 2 pans to the next area.

3 Cameras move away successively. Cam 2 moves first (A to B), then Cam 1 joins it.

95

Changing Shot – Moving Performer

It is all too easy to devise presentations that consist of little more than intercut 'pot-shots' from static viewpoints. But for interest and visual appeal, movement and change are essential.

Performer movement

A long series of static shots can be a bore. Try to introduce some movement of the camera or subject, however slight. Even having someone pointing out details is better than still pictures. When the camera pans as it follows someone around, we get a sense of participation, of anticipation. The picture becomes dynamic. We react to the location.

In longer shots, we are strongly influenced by the surroundings. In closer shots, the performer dominates the picture. So, by varying shot size and performer distance, you can alter visual emphasis.

You can deliberately create 'reasons' for these changes. Talent can *walk* from one item to another, shifting attention to new action areas. They can *gesture* – e.g. pointing over to a feature that the camera zooms in on. They can turn away from the camera, this *body turn* being used to zoom or pan to the next subject. Finally, a *verbal clue* ('Over there we have . . .') is a direct invitation for the shot to change.

Group shots

You can present groups of people in several ways. In a *static* situation (e.g. a discussion) you can selectively shoot individuals, pairs, subgroups, excluding the rest. Intercutting gives shot variety.

Instead of a static arrangement, you can form *changing groups*. These changes are motivated by natural-looking actions. As people sit to make themselves more comfortable, light a cigarette, pour a drink, or fetch a book, they join or leave a group, varying the composition.

Even a gesture can motivate regrouping (illustration opposite):

> Three people are talking. One turns away annoyed (and provides a single shot), while his puzzled neighbor turns towards the third person (forming a two-shot).

By repositioning in this way, you can move people around within the frame, vary the pictorial balance, relocate the center of attention, alter visual emphasis. Regrouping offers fresh shot opportunities that static grouping cannot provide.

Forming shots by isolation
Where people are grouped, and cameras segment the scene into single shots, two-shots, etc., the result is a rather static presentation.

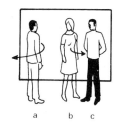

Forming shots by subject movement
People can move 'naturally' to form new groupings. Here, in a three-shot, Person **a** turns away; we cut to CU of him. Person **b** looks towards **c**, to motivate a two-shot.

 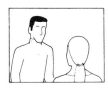

Recomposition by subject movement
The girl confronts her father (her frame position is stronger than his). He rises; the strength of his upward move and new position now make him dominant.

97

Changing Shot – Camera and Switching

When shooting subjects that have little or no movement, you can introduce visual variety by altering the shot or switching.

Changes by camerawork
The simplest way of altering a shot is by zooming or dollying (tracking) to tighten or loosen the framing. So you can readjust the picture, to include or exclude other information; moving in to see detail better (or exclude nearby distractions); moving out to reveal more of the subject or the scene (or introduce additional subjects into the shot).

Although you can modify a shot of a stationary subject by changing camera *height*, or by *arching* round the subject, the effect can look quite cumbersome. When shooting a moving subject, on the other hand, these movements can be very effective; e.g. changing height as someone sits or rises, or arching round as they turn.

Changes by switching
Switching to another camera immediately alters the shot size *(length of shot)*, or relocates the audience's viewpoint. If you change both shot size and direction on the cut, you risk confusing your audience – especially if they cannot recognize their new viewpoint. But if they are prepared for this change (by dialogue or story-line), you can introduce even extreme switches quite unobtrusively (e.g. to an overhead shot, or an entirely different location).

Two very practical hazards encountered in switching are *reverse cuts* and *rediscoveries*. Keep an eagle eye for these when arranging shots as they are disturbing to watch.

Visual changes
When you are showing a series of small objects (vases or statues, perhaps), camera movement alone may not be enough to hold visual interest. Additional techniques that have proved successful include:

- A hand can come into shot, to handle the object (so revealing scale).
- Lighting changes can alter the subject's appearance; varying from silhouette, to texture-revealing side-lighting. Light can be localized, gradually spreading until the complete subject is lit. (Even a painting, or a large piece of statuary, can be treated in this way.)
- You can sometimes 'animate' a subject (where appropriate) by intercutting close shots of details; e.g. in a period painting of a sea battle, interconnecting shots of smoke, falling rigging, guns, firing . . . to a background of battle noises.

98

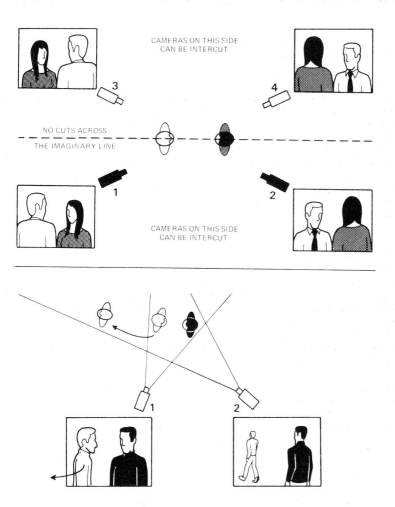

Reverse cuts

Shots can be intercut between cameras located on the same side of an *imaginary line* joining the subjects (1 and 2, 3 and 4). Inter-switching between cameras on *opposite* sides of this line causes the positions of subjects to jump (1 and 3, 1 and 4. 2, and 3. 2 and 4.).

Rediscoveries

If a person exits the frame, it is disconcerting to switch and rediscover them in the next shot. Leaving Cam 1 shot, he reappears on Cam 2.

Shooting the Moving Subject

You can shoot moving subjects in various ways. Each has its own audience impact, and its own problems.

Framing restrictions

Action is difficult to follow in closeup, and where a shot is too tight to contain subject movements, they will pass out of frame. So unless you are content to lose part of the action, you will need a wider shot or a different viewpoint, or must attempt to follow movement. Where action can be anticipated (someone standing or sitting) the camera can usually hold the shot.

Camera movements

Subjects moving to/from the camera are easier to keep in frame than movement across the screen, although diagonal moves are generally the most interesting.

You can follow a move across the scene by panning with it – but there is the hazard that the pan may overreach and shoot beyond the required area. Dollying along beside a moving subject sounds easier than it is in practice. There are other methods, such as cutting at the start of a move to another camera at the destination point, to watch the person arrive, but this can look very contrived, unless really appropriate.

Viewpoint changes

When organizing his camera treatment, a director must always take into account how smoothly and reliably these moves can be carried out. A camera can *creep* imperceptibly closer to a subject while holding a shot. A slow zoom is easier than a *dolly (tracking)* shot, and may suffice instead. *Pulling out* requires rather more skill, and care must be taken not to include unwanted objects nearby as the shot widens. *Arcing* round a subject demands practiced camerawork, particularly if the subject itself is not stationary.

Remember that where a person and a camera are both moving, close coordination is essential, so that the speed of a walk, for example, should be comparable during rehearsals and recording.

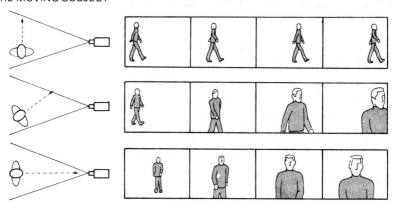

Movement direction

Movements across the screen (a) quickly pass out of shot. Diagonal moves (b) or moves towards the camera (c) can be sustained longer.

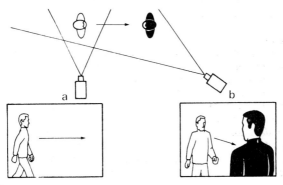

Oblique angles

Movement between widely spaced subjects can only be accommodated on an oblique camera (b).

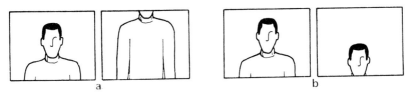

Avoid decapitation

Warn the cameraman of a 'rise' or a 'sit', and avoid bizarre effects.

101

Production Formats

If you compare similar types of program from all over the world, you will find remarkable similarities in the ways they are presented. From formal interviews to cookery demonstrations, from newscasts to talk shows, they appear to have comparable settings, shots, and modes of approach.

Regular formats

Some kinds of production have settled down to a particular format, because this approach works best. Others have become conventions. You could have a weatherman out in the street with an umbrella, or leaping around on a floor map. It has been tried. But in the end, there is much to be said for a person pointing to a map or animated chart. It is less distracting, and simpler, and in the end does the job better.

We could present a quiz show in a lounge setting, with armchairs and sofa, grouped around a TV set; the guests answering the questioner on the screen. Would this be an innovation, or a cranky way of staging a familiar subject? Would it offer the range of shot variations that the more formal method opposite provides? How would the costs and facilities needed compare? Would there be sound pickup or lighting problems? These are the sort of considerations that influence how one presents the subject.

Yesterday's novel approach often becomes today's routine. Changes develop partly through style, and partly through technology. Once *interviews* were invariably formal, and took place in a two-chair or chair-and-desk setup. But now camera and microphone are free to go anywhere. Mobile interviews while walking through city streets or countryside, or in a factory, are now commonplace. In the studio, the deskbound interviewer often talks to someone miles away, through a nearby TV screen, or an electronically inserted picture.

The different approach

So how do we get away from formats and routines? Opinions vary. You can do so by introducing variety. Instead of intercutting static shots, you may introduce *developing shots* that vary the cameras' viewpoints.

Instead of having a garden expert talking direct to camera, someone out of shot can talk to him as we watch him cleaning off his spade, or preparing to sow seeds. Any 'business' that appears to be in character, and naturally motivated, can help to get away from formality, and put the guest at ease.

Be imaginative, but avoid gratuitous gimmicks unless they *really do* add something to the program. Reflections in water, star filters, heavily filtered skies, tapping feet, shooting through prominent foreground flowers . . . quickly become recognizable devices. Fashions come and go!

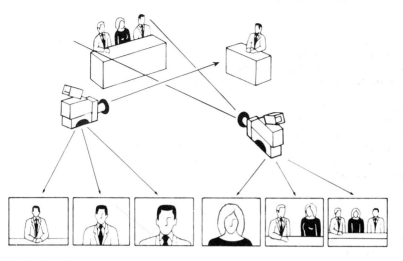

Static shooting
Where cameras are located at *fixed* vantage points and achieve shot variations only by changing lens angles, regular routine treatments often develop.

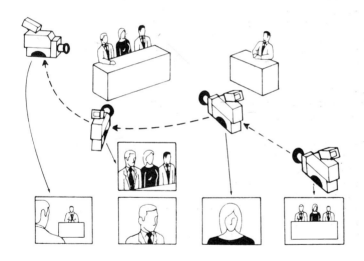

Dynamic shooting
Where camera positions are *varied* to provide viewpoint changes, repetitive shots are readily avoided.

Basic Production Styles

Although TV programs cover a broad spectrum of entertainment, three radical approaches to production techniques are widely used.

The 'stylized routine' approach

This approach works within a systematic framework. However, many a *working format* eventually degenerates into a *stylized routine* that is applied whatever the program subject. Let's look at a typical example:

The show fades up on opening credits.
CUT to a wide shot of the scene, discovering Person 'A'.
CUT to a mid shot of 'A': Who proclaims
  'Hello and good evening!' and introduces Person 'B' . . .
CUT to mid shot of 'B' entering . . . pulling out to a two-shot as 'B' meets up with 'A'.
CUT to closeup of 'A' . . .

We could continue with this kind of shot breakdown ad nauseam . . . and yet, notice that *we've said nothing about the nature of the production itself!* It could be a games show, an interview, a musical recital. The presentation follows a prescribed routine, intercutting wider shots where two or more people are speaking together, with closeups when individuals are making points, or reacting to events. An 'all-purpose' stylized routine!

The 'exploratory' approach

Here picture and sound are used as powerful creative tools; to continually guide the attention, build interest, persuade, intrigue. They stimulate the audience's imagination and influence their emotions. Rather than sitting back passively watching, the audience has an active attitude.

In a drama, we create tension, anxiety and excitement by the way we present the action. A door opens slowly, and a shaft of light begins to spread across the floor of the darkened room. The intruder . . . or just the family pet?

In a documentary, we may encourage our audience to judge the information being presented; to question, debate, compare. We leave them reflecting on the situations they have seen portrayed in the program.

The 'pizazz' approach

Here emphasis is on display; on a rapidly changing succession of images to produce a kaleidoscopic impression. This is the technique used in many video promos. It is associated with energy, vitality, vigor, flair, smartness. It relies on the shock effect of intercutting brief disjointed fragments. The subject appears in a variety of locations. Frames are repeated, stuttering, pixilating, reversed. Slow and fast motion sequences are intercut. Shooting angles change. Backgrounds behind the subject alter rapidly, and are often abstract. Brief clips of material from other sources (e.g. newsreels) are intercut, but have only a tenuous connection with the lyrics. Several pictures of various shapes are simultaneously presented in the frame (notwithstanding squashing or stretching). Images with color changes are superimposed, wiped, intermixed, fragmented and manipulated.

At best, the result can be an exciting outpouring of images, which barely grasp the attention; for there is little time to do more than glance at each, before another takes its place. At worst, it is a pretentious hotch-potch of irrelevant fragments.

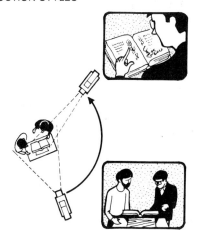

The 'exploratory' approach
The camera moves around the subject to see it from the talent's viewpoint.

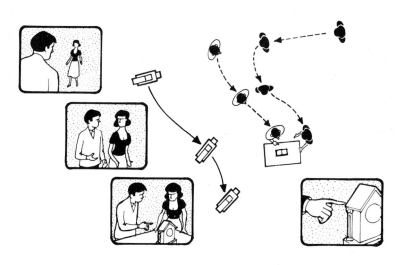

The continually moving camera adds a dynamic element to the action, increasing interest.

105

Developing a TV Production

Here is a general outline of the various stages a large TV production may go through, from the initial idea to the transmitted program.

1 *PROGRAM IDEA*
General assessment of the program idea. Considering how it could be developed and presented.
Where the program material already exists (e.g. a play), enquiries into availability (performance rights, etc.).
Where material is to be prepared and developed, commissioning a writer.
Potential costing. Feasibility assessment. Considering suitable presenters/actors/performers.

2 *RESEARCH*
Research into the subject (gathering data, material availability, etc.).

3 *SCRIPT DEVELOPMENT*
A preliminary script (*draft script/outline script*) may be prepared. This shows the topics to be covered, and the general nature of treatment; perhaps with dialogue, commentary, announcements, etc.

4 *SCRIPT ANALYSIS*
Draft/outline script examined for the order of items/scenes (program running order); possible durations; settings or location shooting required; 'insert' items needed (e.g. library film/videotape), etc.

5 *PRELIMINARY PLANNING*
Director may meet production team principals (cameras, lighting, sound, set designer, etc.) to assess the proposed program format (possible problems, opportunities, etc.).
The designer's rough plans, sketches, samples, are assessed. Preliminary ideas about any special effects (scenic, lighting, video) are discussed.
Initial enquiries may begin about the availability and costs of any special requirements (e.g. hydraulic platform, satellite links, water tanks).

6 *'FINAL' SCRIPT*
Revised script or running order may be prepared, giving finalized information on production treatment.
(Casting, performer booking at this stage.)

7 *PRODUCTION MEETING/TECHNICAL PLANNING*
Firming of production treatment. Here, after the *set designer* has explained the proposed scenic treatment, and the *director* has gone through the show shot by shot, any observations are made by specialists (suggestions, potential problems, changes).
From the 'final script' and provisional set designs, the production team plans and evaluates the technical operations involved:
• Noting performers' positions. General action.
• Considering camera positions, and camera moves.
• Sound pickup arrangements. Positions of sound booms. Sound treatment (music, effects).
• Lighting treatment. Any special effects required.
• Any special scenic effects (e.g. rain) or video effects required.
• The technical facilities needed are assessed.
• Costume and makeup are discussed. (Samples of materials/clothing.)
• Graphics and titling may be discussed.
• The staging plan (setting designs, and their layout in the studio) is agreed.

8   *SPECIALIST ACTIVITIES*
Following the *production meeting* the specialists initiate organization for hiring, contracts, set construction, lighting planning, etc.

9   *REHEARSAL SCRIPT*
'Final script' is prepared, with full details of the action, showing where various effects are required.
(In drama, additional guidance on when/where each scene takes place; e.g. 'Day/Night/Evening'.)
This script, which does not contain technical operational details, is used during all *pre-studio rehearsals*, and for general production organization.

10   *PRE-STUDIO REHEARSALS*
(Typically in a rehearsal hall before the studio session.) Actors/performers practice dialogue (lines), the action, business, their moves.

11   *CAMERA SCRIPT*
This script is a composite, developed by adding extra details to the original *rehearsal script*.
It contains all technical operational details, including information on camera positions and moves, switching, audio details, cues, etc.

12   *TECHNICAL RUN*
A final pre-studio rehearsal. Attended by specialists (cameras, lighting, sound) to familiarize themselves with the action and treatment, and check for possible operational or staging problems.

13   *PREPARE STUDIO*
Set up and light scenery, dress settings – arrange furniture, hang drapes, position ornaments, properties, rugs, etc.
Assemble the camera and sound equipment.
Check that videotape, film and slide channels have any insert material required for the show. Check all titling.

14   *CAMERA REHEARSALS*
Action is rehearsed, while the camera crew, sound crew, electricians, stage hands etc. follow the director's instructions (over intercom/talkback).
Floor manager oversees and controls studio activities.

15   *RECORDING SESSION*
The program may be recorded in sections, or in its entirety.

16   *OFF-LINE EDITING*
The director (and/or VT editor) examines a compact VCR unedited copy of a videotape of the production, which displays *on-screen timecode* throughout, to identify shots. Guided by notes made during taping session, the director decides on the selection and order of shots, potential editing points, types of transitions, etc. Also considers where after-treatment is needed to complete/improve production (e.g. added effects, music, etc.).

17   *ON-LINE EDITING*
Sequences are copied from the original videotapes and sound, in the required final order, to form a *show copy*.
Any corrections in the picture (e.g. color balance) or sound (filtering, reverberation) are made.
Titles, audio effects, background music, video effects etc. are added.

18   *REVIEW*
Final version ('show copy') of the composite tape is checked and passed.
Airing/transmission schedule confirmed.
Promotion.

19   *TRANSMISSION*
Final tape may be copied for distribution, archives.

In smaller productions, these various steps may be abbreviated or missed out altogether. For example, an INTERVIEW would not require steps 2–6, 9, 10, 12, (16).

Planning Visual Treatment

Where you position cameras to get the best shot opportunities largely depends on the subject and the action. But there are certainly two *very poor* general approaches:

• *Continuous straight-on shots*. Here you set up the camera directly in front of the subject, and rely on zoom lens adjustments to vary the shot size. The result can be mechanical and quite boring to watch. Sometimes, two frontal cameras are used side by side, intercutting wide and close shots; but again, this can produce very routine results.

Where you have to shoot continuous action with *one camera*, you can create visual variety by frequent changes in shot size *and* camera viewpoint.

• *Trial and error*. Here the director moves the camera around experimentally, seeking an attractive angle, then readjusts the subject and background for the best composition. This empirical approach can work for a static subject, but is very time-consuming. If you then alter the shot or switch to another camera angle, it can upset the whole effect!

Instead, it is far better to adopt either a *planned viewpoints* or a *storyboard* approach.

Planned viewpoints

In this widely used method, cameras are located at strategic points overlooking the action.

In a *three-camera production*, one is usually located front-center with two cross-shooting cameras on either side. One camera mainly concentrates on long to medium shots, while others take medium to close shots. Shot sizes are varied to suit the action.

Well handled, this approach can provide very practical effective results. Rehearsal is uncomplicated, for the cameras do not move far from their 'home positions', and their shots are easily coordinated. Where the action is spontaneous or unpredictable, camera operators may offer up 'good shots', and the switcher cuts to whichever is most appropriate.

When cameras continually move around the action area, shots need to be worked out carefully in advance, to avoid cameras seeing each other, overshooting, reversed cuts, poor visual continuity, etc.

Storyboard approach

This is a systematic planned approach. The director thinks through the production, drawing rough sketches showing what he/she wants to see in each *key shot*; then works out how the cameras need to be positioned and moved to achieve them. For example:

The man confronts the boy who has just broken a window. The frames opposite show the treatment, and the camera moves needed to build up this picture sequence.

108

Planned viewpoints
Cameras are placed in positions from which they can get clear shots of the action. Their pictures are intercut as required.

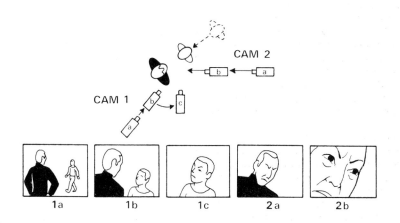

Storyboard approach
A dramatic action sequence is conceived as a series of sketched frames. The camera treatment is then devised to provide these pictures.

109

Shot Development

When organizing a scene, you need to consider not only how you are going to arrange each key shot, but how it is going to develop into subsequent shots.

Setting up the shot
Preferably using a *'normal' lens angle* of around 20–27°, adjust the camera's *distance* from the subject, to give you the shot size you want – e.g. a waist shot. Although you could simply alter the zoom lens' angle instead, remember that this will exaggerate or compress depth to some extent. (*Slight* changes in lens angle to tighten or loosen the shot a little will not be noticed.)
   Choose the camera's *height* to suit the situation.
- *Higher viewpoints* diminish the subject's strength or importance, and reveal more of the floor and middle distance.
- *Lower viewpoints* do the opposite, and foreground objects become more prominent, while the middle distance becomes foreshortened.

Arrange the shot's *framing* to provide the most effective composition making sure that the *headroom* is appropriate.

Changing the viewpoint
When you record shots one at a time, you can modify each a little if necessary ('cheat') for the best effect. But remember that rearranging any shot may upset its continuity with previous ones.
   When you *move* a camera from one viewpoint to another, there are no problems with visual continuity. But when you *switch* to a new viewpoint, there is always the possibility that this will produce a disturbing visual upset (e.g. a jump cut). To avoid this happening, you can:
- *Use equalized viewpoints.* Arrange subjects so that they look good from several directions.
- *Readjust people's positions as the shot changes.* You cut as they can move on a *word cue* ('Come in' . . . he turns towards the door), or on an *action cue* (as she sits), or on *'business'* (as he puts down the glass).

   Carefully done, the action will appear continuous; even when pictures shot at different times and places are cut together. Cut from someone at a window to a person in the street looking up, and you have a relationship where none actually existed!

Developing shots
Here, instead of intercutting static viewpoints, we move the camera around within the scene. This not only gives the audience a strong subjective feeling, as if they were taking part in the action, but conveys a clearer idea of layout and positions than when intercutting cameras. However, it does require skilled, carefully controlled camerawork.
   Its *slow pace* makes the developing shot particularly effective in building up tension, when creating expectancy, or when you are shooting solemn occasions.

110

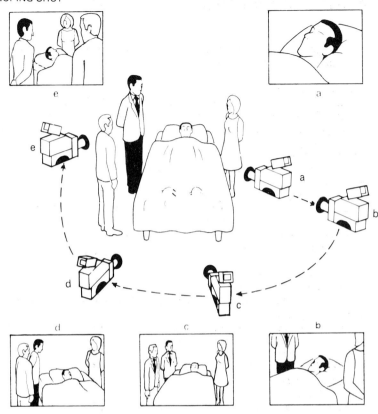

Developing shot
In this bedside scene, intercutting would have disrupted the solemn mood. And
yet you want to show various reactions, and create continuous visual interest.
This slow developing shot provides movement which is unobtrusive, yet
contrasting with the stillness of the scene.

111

Pictorial Variety

An effective production attracts and holds audience interest. It carefully concentrates and relaxes their attention. It avoids the predictable, and may even include an element of surprise. It avoids a succession of routine repetitive shots. There is continual *variety*

Introducing variety
Variety through design – One of the problems one faces in presenting most TV programs is that *it has all been done before!* But even where shows have an everyday familiarity (such as interviews, newscasters, demonstrations), you can give them a fresh interesting look through careful scenic treatment.

Variety through movement – Movement arouses interest, and creates pictorial variety. But movement that does not seem to have any *purpose*, however slight, is obtrusive. When someone stands up and takes a book from a nearby shelf, they appear to be *motivated*. When the camera goes in to look at the book, this move too seems to have a purpose. Introduce too much movement, though, and the result can look fidgety or contrived.

Variety through changes in viewpoint – If you hold the shot from a fixed viewpoint for too long, the audience's interest falls. They feel that their view of the action is restricted. When you change the camera viewpoint, they see fresh aspects of the action and the surroundings, and you give them a sense of visual freedom.

Variety through changes in shot size – Broadly speaking, *close shots* concentrate the attention, *medium length shots* show responses between people, while *longer shots* establish where the action is taking place. By using a blend of these different shot qualities, you create pictorial variety.

Variety through visual effects – Almost endless numbers of visual gimmicks are available at the touch of a button. The temptation is to use them – even when they are not really appropriate! Some can be used for *serious* purposes (e.g. a multi-image screen showing what is happening in several different places), or for a fun effect. Make sure the audience understands which you intend!

Variety through camera techniques – Selective camera techniques can create striking pictorial changes. *Pull focus* from foreground barbed wire to the prisoners beyond, and you have a powerful symbolic image. Do the same from foreground flowers to a car traveling along the highway, and it's just a meaningless visual gimmick.

112

Pictorial variety
By the ways in which we arrange people in a shot, we can create visual variety,
concentrate attention, and suggest prevailing mood.

113

What Facilities Are Needed?

It is generally better to build up from basic production treatment that will work effectively, than to start with a complex idea that has to be considerably simplified.

A matter of degree
Most subjects can be presented in a number of quite different ways, some more successful than others. But remember, elaboration does not guarantee a better program – often the reverse. Take a subject such as 'Warfare'.

- Presentation could be very basic – a seated storyteller.
- You might include illustrations . . . stills . . . graphics . . . film clips . . . miniature layouts showing battles.
- Given the budget, animated film, dramatic reenactments . . . even location battles!

But do these make your points better? They may, but on the other hand they might introduce an unnecessary and costly over-gloss instead!

Alternative methods
You can often use several quite different methods to achieve the same effect. Some are easier or more flexible to use than others. A high shot that would really need a camera crane may be obtained by putting a camera on an elevated area (parallels, rostra, frame tower), by shooting into a suspended mirror, or even by cutting to a photo-still taken earlier.

A special facility used for one brief shot alone is usually wasteful of time and effort. But a whole scene might require special treatment, such as shots from ground level throughout. If so, are special low level dollies necessary, or can the problem be overcome by arranging the action on an elevated area, and using normal floor pedestals?

Tempting facilities
Various facilities have become widely available, so that the temptation is to use them – because they are there. Resist the temptation! Think twice before using a *wipe, whip-pan, zoom, star filters, superimposition, synthesized color*. They may all be there at the touch of a switch, but are they *appropriate*?

What does the viewer see?
The audience cares little about how difficult or costly it is to achieve a given shot. They are only concerned with the *effect*. If the camera looks through a doorway and apparently sees a room interior, it is not important that this 'room' is really only made from a couple of scenic flats. Carefully chosen camera viewpoints can prove economical in staging and facilities. Judiciously used chromakey (CSO), too, can provide elaborate effects with minimum staging. Although such approaches may preclude interesting developing shots, they can provide considerable visual variety.

114

Coping without facilities

There will always be times when a program maker's ambition has to be limited by facilities, budget, time, space, manpower and so on. But by using a little ingenuity, you can often get round these problems. Even when shooting live, difficulties can arise that have quite simple solutions. Here are a few regular examples of ways in which you may create greater visual flexibility than your situation would normally allow.

Too few cameras ● Restrict the amount of action in the scene, and the area of movement, so that the camera(s) can shoot effectively. ● In a two-camera setup, arrange for one of the cameras to move away before the end of the scene, to the next location, ready for the next scene. ● Videotape each section/scene separately, concentrating all available cameras there. ● Introduce shots of slides, graphics, film, or videotape, to allow you to move your main studio camera(s) to new positions.

Cameras immobile ● Where your camera cannot move around (static tripod, uneven ground, very distant from subject to shoot on a narrow angle lens), arrange the action and subject distances to suit simple panning and zooming. Have the performers work to the camera, changing distance to vary the shot. ● If the camera cannot go in to see the detail, cut to inserts (photographs, slides, or videotape) of the detail, shot separately. ● Either pan, or pull focus between a series of carefully positioned items. ● Occasionally, it is possible to pan from a subject to a nearby mirror reflecting a different scene.

Lens angle is fixed ● When you are using a fixed lens angle (i.e. not a zoom lens) you can introduce a great deal of visual mobility by varying the distance of the performers from the camera, and by moving the camera around to follow the action. Wherever possible, have the performers move to give a 'reason' for the camera to dolly, e.g. to follow as someone walks from one spot to another. ● If another lens is not available for particular narrow angle or wide angle effects, clip on an additional, supplementary lens ('negative' for a narrower angle; 'positive' for a wider angle).

Insufficient time to move a camera ● If during a two-camera live program there is too little time at the conclusion of the first scene for the second camera to move to its new shot elsewhere, the first scene can be 'stretched' by adding extra dialogue or things for performers to do at its end (action, business). ● Introduce cutaway shots of graphics or slides to bridge the transition.

Limited space ● Use wide angle lenses to exaggerate space. ● Change the appearance of a setting (revamp) so that it can be reused during the show: by replacing furniture, wall decoration, drapes, etc; or by relighting. ● Shoot set from a different angle. ● Use small 'partial' settings in which although only a localized area is used, the effect suggests a much more extensive arrangement. ● Where a studio setting has windows, cover them with nets or drapes, then space-occupying backings will not be needed. Similarly, avoid using doors, or hinge them downstage. ● Use chromakey (or front projection), or realistic backdrops (e.g. photo blowups) to suggest extensive locations. ● By shooting via a mirror, you can lengthen the effective shooting distance, and the width of shot. ● You can introduce false (forced) perspective in the setting for an illusion of greater space. ● If two or more small settings have similar decor, when cameras are intercut between them, their combined shots will suggest one large area.

Limited staging resources ● See 'Limited space'. ● Use adaptable or reversible scenery (i.e. slip-aside panels; turn-over flats; pull-aside drapes, rear-projected patterns on translucent panels, etc.). ● Use a cyclorama as a universal background, with projected light patterns, shadows, pin-on motifs, foreground standing pieces, etc. ● Augment standard plain flats with drapes on lightweight frames.

Limited lighting facilities ● Where you have few lamps, restrict the area seen in shot and concentrate available light there. Light and record one scene at a time. ● Use chromakey to simulate background/setting, using lighting for color backdrop (keying color) and people. ● To suggest lighting wall shading or shadows where facilities are limited, airbrush or paint the effects.

No slide or film island ● Project the film image onto a screen (shield off any spill-light) and shoot with a video camera.

Is Planning Really Necessary?

Planning involves your making decisions, organizing, and coordinating the various elements that contribute to the production.

Unplanned production
For simple productions, it is possible with experience and a modicum of luck to 'work things out as you go', and create from scratch on the day. While scenery is being erected and lit, you walk the camera and sound crew round the setting, explaining the action and probable shots, and then rehearse.

But don't rely on this approach. At best it is makeshift. If you suddenly decide that you need three matching chairs instead of two, or a low glass-topped table, they may not be available unless you happen to have a sizeable property store to draw on.

Even where you cannot organize in detail beforehand, you can still develop a working scheme to relate to.

No need to plan
When a production follows a regular recurrent format, such as a daily talks show, and everyone involved is familiar with the shots and action, continual planning is not really necessary. Just inform the team of any variations or differences in that day's show.

Plan to make it happen
Planning may seem at first to be a restrictive chore. But it pays dividends! Without a clear idea of how you want to present your subject, and some preliminary planning, you have an empty studio, or a crew wondering what to do! If you rely on happenstance, results will be unpredictable, and usually disappointing. The end product could even prove to be a sad waste of time, money and effort.

Planning principles
Careful planning helps the director to work out how he/she is going to treat the subject in picture and sound, and to arrange talent and facilities to achieve this.

The basis of most planning is typically:
- A *script* (full or outline) giving details of the production.
- A *running order* showing the order of scenes, items or acts.
- A *scale plan* of the studio, with outlines of proposed settings.
- *Sketches* and/or a *storyboard* giving a pictorial idea of the shots and treatment.

Well in advance of the scheduled rehearsal/recording dates, the director meets with the various specialists responsible for all aspects of the production, and outlines his/her ideas. They in turn offer their individual expertise, evaluate and extend these ideas, anticipate problems, and go on to organize their contributions to the show.

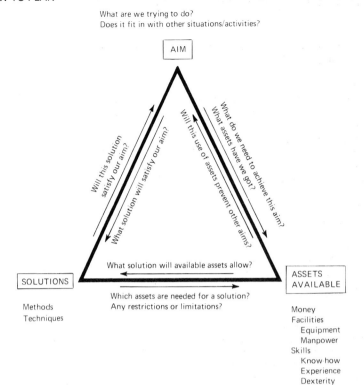

What are we trying to do?
Does it fit in with other situations/activities?

AIM

What do we need to achieve this aim?
What assets have we got?

Will this solution satisfy our aim?

What solution will satisfy our aim?

Will this use of assets prevent other aims?

What solution will available assets allow?

SOLUTIONS

What solution will available assets allow?

Which assets are needed for a solution?
Any restrictions or limitations?

Methods
Techniques

ASSETS
AVAILABLE

Money
Facilities
　Equipment
　Manpower
Skills
　Know-how
　Experience
　Dexterity
Time available

The planning process
The problem is *where to begin!* This 'universal problem-solving circuit' helps us to think coherently about planning procedures. Whenever we have a problem, we must relate any potential solution to our assets, or the result will be unsuccessful. Note how the circuit works clockwise and anti-clockwise. There is often no *correct* solution, only an optimum for your needs.

Production Approaches

Directors vary in the ways they tackle their productions.

Unplanned production
Those who can't visualize action and shots unless it's all happening in front of them tend to avoid the commitment of planning as far as possible. During rehearsal, they arrange action, then choose shots (often promoted by the camera crew), which they intercut and blend into a free-flowing presentation. Results can vary from exciting, dynamic spontaneity . . . to bewildering chaos.

For some kinds of production (e.g. documentaries), there is a temptation to shoot any promising material, which is later selected and arranged into a coherent program, while 'junking' all unwanted sequences. With luck, the result is a fresh uninhibited approach. At worst, it's just a ragbag of disjointed shots, strung together with visual effects and music.

Sometimes you may have little choice but to record whatever material is available, rather than organize matters as you want them. But wherever possible, it's best to work out even a rough *storyline* or *treatment* beforehand, to provide a systematic shooting plan to which you can relate the shots.

Outline planning
Especially when using several cameras, effective production comes from systematic planning, seasoned with a touch of on-the-spot inspiration, and unexpected opportunities.

Occasionally there is no time for detailed planning. You learn that your live show now has an unexpected unrehearsed extra item. Then the only solution is to prepare an immediate outline framework that is likely to suit the situation. This might simply consist of:
- Checking the most suitable area that can be lit quickly.
- Arranging scenic treatment (e.g. dropping in drapes).
- Positioning any major items needed (e.g. chairs, table).
- Allocating typical shots to cameras: *either general indications* such as 'Cam 1 covers broad action; Cam 2 takes close shots' *or specific shots* such as 'Cam 1 takes long shot of the entrance; Cam 2 a mid shot of the host greeting the guest'.
- Organizing the sound pickup.

In most cases, though, you can analyze the situation beforehand, and then position the camera(s) to give the best coverage.

Working to a script
You can script a production at several levels.
An *outline script* just indicates
- Scheduled times for rehearsal, meals, recording, etc.
- Details of the production team/crew involved.
- Equipment required (e.g. cameras, sound, etc.).
- Participants'/performers' names.
- Any introductory announcements, commentary.
- Basic information on action.

The crew makes notes of shots/action arranged during rehearsal, and uses these (together with intercom prompting) during the recording session.

When a *full script* is used, this includes all the dialogue, and provides a detailed plan of action for the performers, cameras and sound, with guidance for lighting and scenic changes, special effects, etc.

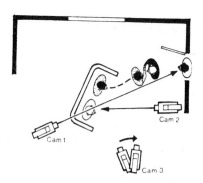

Treatment breakdown
This plan shows a typical shot breakdown for a brief scene.
The positions shown may represent
      three separate cameras,
or   *two* cameras (one at 'Cam 1' position, another moving from 'Cam 2'
      to 'Cam 3' positions).
or   *one* camera shooting with three setups.

Shot 1: Cam 3 — Mid-shot of man and woman talking on sofa. Doorbell rings.
              Man rises to open door . . . CAMERA PANS
Shot 2: CUT to Cam 1 as door opens to reveal child (waist shot).
Shot 3: CUT to Cam 2 — Mid-shot showing woman's reaction (surprise).
Shot 4: CUT to Cam 1 — Shot over woman's shoulder of man and child.
Shot 5: CUT to Cam 3 — Long shot of group. Child walks to woman, shot
              tightening to two-shot.
Shot 6: CUT to Cam 1 — Mid-shot of man (smiling), who sits . . .

Organizing Production Mechanics

Planning and organizing processes vary from one establishment to the next. In a small studio, everyone combines forces to build the show, and job demarcations are slight. At a larger studio center, interdepartmental and union relationships are usually clear-cut, and a considerable amount of documentation is necessary for the wheels to turn. Whatever the system, the people who are going to provide the various facilities and services still have to discuss their respective ideas. The list on the facing page is a reminder of the scope for discussion.

Production resources
However experienced, a director cannot hope to know the answers to the thousand and one aspects that arise when devizing a TV show. That is why he has expert advice from specialists. Some apparently difficult requirements are remarkably easy to meet (such as a shot of a man suddenly shrinking to become minute), while paradoxically, some 'simple' situations can pose real problems as for example obtaining convincing open-air acoustics in large-area studio scenes. So the director consults his aides on how to obtain a convincing illusion, how to save money and time, how a setting can be modified to offer a better variety of shots and so on.

Will it work?
In practical terms, planning usually prompts the question: What are we trying to achieve? How can we accomplish this? Will that method work? Are there any potential problems? How do we overcome these? Was the idea a good one in the first place? Many a 'great idea' has proved to be a confounded nuisance to other contributing specialists, or an unworkable fiasco on the studio floor. The more we can anticipate and rationalize at the planning stage, the better.

Take a simple example of aspects discussed for a scene:

> *A girl walks upstairs, speaking throughout the walk.* How is the camera shooting the walk? It is tilting up from a position at the foot of the stairs. Will the camera shoot off the top of the set? No, there is a ceiling. Will this ceiling preclude appropriate lighting? No, it can be effectively lit from these other directions. If a sound boom is to follow the walk, the boom operator will not be able to see from the suggested position. Then a flat must be moved to give him a clear view. The mike might be seen in the long shot. Can't the mike work further away for that shot? The sound quality (acoustics) will change, particularly due to the low ceiling. Let's see if it is too bad, or if we have to use other sound pickup methods. Will the footsteps on the stairs sound authentic? They are thickly carpeted, so that should be all right.

Camera cable routing, too, is a potential hazard. Cables can get snarled up, or block other cameras' moves, or drag around making noises. Many directors therefore move scale cut-outs on cords around their *staging plan*, to ascertain problems, before allocating camera positions for their *camera plan*.

Typical considerations in technical planning

Outline – Director outlines the nature of the production, style, general indication of techniques to be used (e.g. single camera, multi-camera, rehearse/record, live-on-tape, etc.).

Talent – Discusses particular requirements of talent, *re* costume, makeup (styles, fitting arrangements, etc.).

Staging – Set designer describes the proposed style, layout, and treatment of settings. On a staging plan (perhaps with a card model) details of the set structures are discussed (as they affect available shots, lighting, sound pickup). Any scenic changes are agreed (*re*: settings revamped, repositioned, moved, dismantled, erected during the production). Arrangements for storage of props, standby scenery, in the studio during the show. Audience seating.

Any effects involved in the production, ranging from *physical effects* (e.g. simulating snow, smoke, fire, etc.) to *lighting effects* (e.g. lightning, firelight, etc.), and *video effects* (e.g. chromakey backgrounds).

Check up on any safety precautions required, staging restrictions (e.g. maximum floor weight), etc.

Action – Director outlines where he anticipates performers will stand, the nature of action, and any special business involved. (These may affect the way the setting is constructed, how action is lit, shooting problems, sound treatment, etc.).

Cameras – Director indicates the number of cameras required; types of camera mountings; the main camera positions in each scene; and probable camera moves.

Any special camera accessories needed (e.g. lens filters, effects attachments).

Specialists evaluate the proposed treatment, anticipating equipment requirements, possible problems, etc. (e.g. sufficient working space, time for moves, camera cable routing, etc.).

Lighting – The lighting director examines the staging arrangements and the proposed production treatment (camera shots, audio) and considers probable lighting treatment. (Taking into account time available, lighting equipment, manpower, lamp-rigging problems, safety, etc.) He discusses with the director and set designer such factors as the colors, tones, etc. of settings, pictorial effects, atmosphere, mood, etc., picture-matching to film or videotape inserts.

Audio – Discussion on audio pickup problems, mike arrangements, the need for recorded sound inserts (music, effects).

Video effects – Planning of chromakey (CSO) or other video effects.

Graphics, titles – Arrangements for all artwork, displays, etc.

Further technical facilities – Organizing facilities for any pre-studio filming or videotaping. Also technical resources needed for the studio production; e.g. studio floor monitors, prompters, film island (telecine, slide scanner), videotape, recording channel, etc.

Scheduling – Arrangements for *pre-studio shooting* (filming, videotape, audio recording, etc.). Any experimental sessions.

Pre-studio rehearsals – Preliminary script read-through; blocking action; rehearsal of lines/action. ('Technical run-through' for technicians/operators to assess operations.)

Studio activities – Preparation and erection of settings, set dressing. Lighting rigging and setting lamps. Rehearsal and recording periods (rehearse and record in sequences, in scenes, or straight through).

Post-production – Editing. Post-production dubbing, etc.

Plans and Elevations

Two major documents form the basis of studio production planning – the *staging plan/floor plan* and *scenic elevations*.

The studio plan

The empty *studio plan* is a standard scale drawing of the entire studio – typically to a metric scale of 1:50; i.e. 2 cm = 1 m. (Formerly ¼ in to 1 ft scale was used.) Printed on tracing paper, it may show such features as:

- The location of *storage areas*, and *service areas* (makeup, changing rooms, etc.).
- All *entrances/exits*, scenic loading bay, stairways, access points, etc.
- The *staging area* within which scenery can be erected.
- The 1 m/3 ft wide *safety lane (fire lane)* around the studio.
- The positions of various general *supplies*; e.g. gas, water, power.
- The positions of all *outlets/technical supplies* for camera, sound, lighting.
- The location of *overhead lighting support systems* (battens, rails, etc.).
- The position of the *cyclorama* support rails.
- Data on heights, weight-carrying capacities, sizes, etc.

How the studio plan is used

From the studio plan, major reference documents are derived:

- *The staging plan (floor plan, ground plan, setting plan)*. The *set designer/ scenic designer* draws scale outlines of settings ('sets') on the studio plan. In a complex production, sets drawn on individual *tracing overlays* are readjusted for optimum camera, lighting and sound access.
- *Furniture/props plan*. This is a detailed plan of a setting, showing where furniture, decorations, drapes, are to be placed.
- *The camera plan (production plan)*. The director draws on a copy of the *staging plan*, the numbered positions of all cameras and sound booms, perhaps with indications of camera cable routes. This *camera plan* is used at the *production planning meeting* when the director explains the envisioned camera treatment.

   The *camera plan* is also used by the camera crew and sound crew, before and during rehearsal, to guide them in positioning their equipment.
- *The lighting plot* may be drawn on a copy of the camera plan, or on a separate tracing overlay. Lighting fitting symbols are drawn in their required 'rigged positions', with details of power supply channels, accessories, color media, etc.

Elevations

Elevations show side-on views of all scenery to the same scale as the staging plan. They give details of all vertical structures' construction and finish (walls, staircases, etc.). Used primarily by construction workshops, and the crew setting up the scenery, they help all members of the team to imagine what the actual scenery will look like when erected.

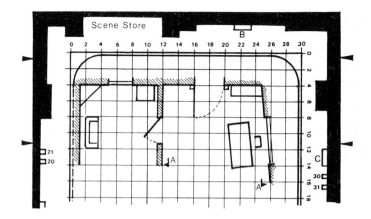

The staging plan
Scale outlines of settings are
drawn on the studio plan.

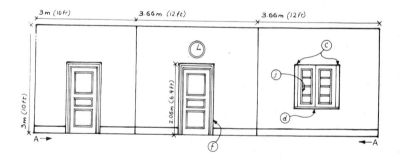

Elevations
These show details of all vertical structures. The sizes, style, finish of walls,
together with details of special features, are included (c, d, f, j).

123

Developing the Staging Plan

Let's look at a typical approach when designing a *staging plan/floor plan/setting plan*.

Organizing the studio layout
• First break the production down into its basic scenes, acts, or sequences (check the running order).
• How many settings are needed?
• Are any used more than once? Can any be reused from different angles, or revamped for other scenes?
• Sketch scale plans of possible designs for settings, showing the main features (windows, doors, staircases, etc.) on pieces of tracing paper. Check that they really are to scale; e.g. no 'miniature furniture' suggesting that there is plenty of space.
• Arrange these scale overlays of settings around the studio plan in the shooting order – to avoid unnecessary moves between sets.
• Check the overall size and working area of each setting. If it is too cramped or small, action and the shot variety will be restricted. Cameras may overshoot. But if action is very limited (e.g. someone using a phone) a single scenic flat may suffice.
• If necessary, adjust the position and shape of each setting, to allow easy access:
  for cameras (e.g. to shoot through windows),
  for sound (e.g. check nothing impedes the sound boom),
  for lighting (e.g. space to light a cyclorama).
• An 'operational zone' is needed in front of each setting to allow camera and booms to be positioned and maneuver around.
• Allow sufficient space within settings to suit the action.
• Consider the amount of space required for, for example, seating. Is there really room for 10 people playing instruments on the platform?
• If cameras are likely to move about *within* a setting, leave room for dolly movements. (No rugs or uneven floor in these areas.)
• Allow space for performers to enter/leave settings; i.e. access steps to platforms, offstage space behind doorways.
• Large settings only offer good production value in long shots, or where action is widespread; but not in closer shots.
• Allocate floor space for temporary storage during production, (for movable scenery, properties, standby items, graphics, title stands, picture monitors, loudspeakers).
• Consider studio access from nearby storage areas, for technical equipment. Keep safety/fire lanes clear of scenery.

Will it work?
The director and designer examine the staging plan to check out shot potentials: 'If the flat at the end of this wall is hinged ('swinger') it will allow better camera access.' 'A cross-shooting camera might see past the end of the set, let's have some extended flattage there.' 'We need something in the foreground here, to improve the feeling of depth.'
And so many problems are caught before they even happen. Last-minute alterations are avoided, and precious rehearsal time is saved.

124

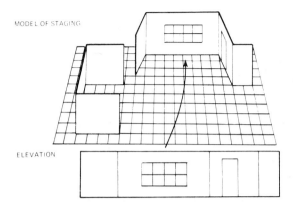

MODEL OF STAGING

ELEVATION

The staging model

The scale *model* is made in card from *elevations* of the setting stuck on a plan. It shows basic structural and surface details.

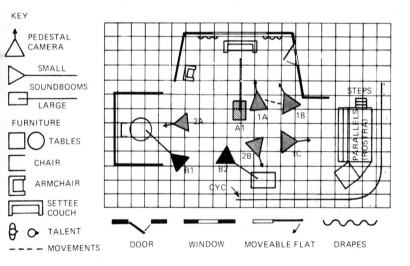

KEY

PEDESTAL CAMERA

SMALL SOUNDBOOMS

LARGE

FURNITURE

TABLES

CHAIR

ARMCHAIR

SETTEE COUCH

TALENT

MOVEMENTS

DOOR   WINDOW   MOVEABLE FLAT   DRAPES

The camera plan

The staging plan shows the settings distributed around the setting area, together with their furniture. Cameras and sound-boom positions are indicated. (Booms: A1,B1,2. Cameras: 1A,B,C. 2A,B.)

Planning Shots

No director *creates* with a protractor and squared paper. He thinks in terms of *pictures* – of visual arrangements that produce a particular effect or mood. But good shots, coupled with smooth compositional continuity, do not just happen. They need forethought and planning. With experience, 'guesstimates' can be made. Real accuracy requires scale calculations. But they are a creative aid, not a substitute for imaginative thought.

Working it out

Paper planning saves studio rehearsal time. Moreover ideas can be worked out in private, without having to trundle dollies around to see what will happen. The tools are a scale plan, and a transparent triangle representing the lens angle (an adjustable protractor is ideal).

The principles involved are quite simple. The angle at the apex of the transparent triangle is the same as the horizontal angle of the camera lens to be used (e.g. 25°). Wherever it is placed on the studio plan, it shows the same field of view as covered by the studio camera with its lens positioned at the apex. When the angle does not fall within the set, then the camera will be shooting off if set up at that point in the studio.

Shot proportions

The lines that form the angle represent the left and right edges of the screen. If an object is positioned so that it touches both of the lines, it exactly fills the screen width – whether it is a small close object, or a large distant one.

Suppose an object is required to fill *a certain proportion of the screen width* (say, one third). Multiply the object's width by that proportion (e.g. 3) and, taking a piece of paper of this marked length, move it until it fits. The object will then appear to fill one third of the shot width. Suppose the subject is a person (full face is ⅜ in wide on a ¼ in scale, for a person is roughly 18 inches across the shoulders*). To fill one third of the screen with a person full-faced, move a 3 × ⅜ in marker until it fills the angle. On a 25° lens, the measured result is 3½ ft away.

Opposite is a quick shot check for a 25° lens. This shows all the subject distances at which the standard shots can be obtained with a 25° lens. If you are using another lens angle, multiply the table distance by that factor:

$$50° = ½. \quad 10° = 2.5. \quad 40° = \frac{25}{40} \text{ (i.e. 0.6)}.$$

* 1:50 is 2 cm = 1 m. Metric scale: People are roughly 0.45 metre across, 0.25 deep.

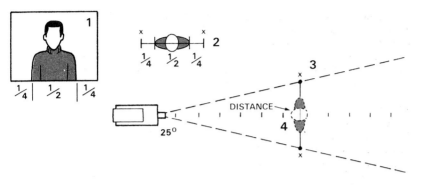

How can we get this shot?

Check your scale used. (If ¼ in = 1 ft, a man is ⅜ in across.)   1. How much of shot does he occupy (e.g. ½).   2. Draw scale line with man ½ its length.   3. Fit line across lens angle (at X−X).   4. Read distance needed to get shot.

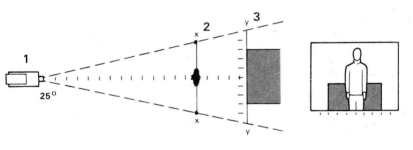

SHOT	BCU	CU HEAD/SHLDRS.	MCU CHEST	MID-SHOT WAIST	¾ SHOT KNEES	FULL LENGTH
FT.	3	4	5.5	7	14	+20
M.	0.86	1.27	1.72	2.10	4.26	+6.08

What does this setup give?

Man is 14 ft away on 25° lens, therefore: This is a ¾-shot (*knee shot*) in table below. For any item, draw line across angle at that point (e.g. X−X). This shows shot width at that distance. What proportion of shot is occupied by desk? Desk is at Y−Y, 6 units wide. Shot width 10 units at that point, therefore desk fills $^6/_{10}$ = 0.6 of screen.

127

Scripting for Television

For most productions, a good script is the underlying framework for the whole operation.

Script formats
You can arrange scripts in two ways:
- *Single-column.* A single-column layout, similar to that used for film scripts. All dialogue and action details are in a wide central column. Director's notes on cameras' shots and switching are handwritten in the left margin.
- *Dual-column.* A more comprehensive, information two-column arrangement (see example opposite) has *picture information* on the left, with *sound information* (dialogue, sound effects, etc.) and action on the right.

When is it written?
The script for most productions is written beforehand, and forms a reference document for all planning, rehearsal and recording. It is modified slightly as necessary.

Documentary-type programs depend considerably on what is available when shooting. So they work to a *guide outline* or *draft script*. The main script is written later, to coordinate the material.

Script style
With many subjects the *picture* predominates. Dialogue and music extend the picture's significance, explaining and augmenting what is seen. With other subjects, the *sound* predominates. What is being said (or played) is most important, and is supported by the pictures.

Script style depends on your intended audience. How you develop ideas will vary with the time available, and the elaboration called for. Script style should always relate to the *spoken word*, not the *written page*. Don't address individuals as if speaking to a public meeting. Overcomplicated ideas obscure thought. Simple words and short sentences are best.

Getting the ideas across
The more complex the subject, the more important it is to approach it in easy stages. Your audience can't turn back to recognize and understand the significance of each point. Their *assimilation rate* will vary with the subject's familiarity and complexity. Information may need an introduction, and finally a summary. Make one point at a time, and avoid giving too many facts, too quickly. Development should be gradual and progressive. Don't repeat points unnecessarily. Where several topics are shown simultaneously, or rapidly intercut, the audience can become confused.

Script mechanics
Any script has to be *practicable*. In a live show, you may need to anticipate studio operations; e.g. writing extra dialogue, to give a camera time to move. When commenting to film or tape, you may need carefully timed pauses to avoid words out-racing the picture. Or extra words may be needed to cover long action. It is better for an explanation to slightly precede the picture, rather than lag behind it while the audience wonders what the shot is all about.

CAMS. 1B, 2D, 3C.   SOUND BOOMS A3, B4.

3.   INT.   KITCHEN   DAY

20.   2   D
BCU PAT'S hands,
showing counting
coins.
PULL BACK SLOWLY,
to CU stopping at
door knock.

(PAT IS SEATED AT
TABLE, A BOX BEFORE HIM,
FROM WHICH HE TAKES GOLD
COINS. HE COUNTS AND
PILES THEM. THERE IS A
KNOCK AT THE DOOR.)

PAT: What do you want? (INCOHERENT
SOUND FROM OUTSIDE DOOR)

21.   1   B
BCU Door latch
ZOOM OUT to MS as
door opens.

Who's there, I say!
(THUMPING ON DOOR.
DOOR LATCH RISES. A
BODY FALLS IN, ONTO
THE FLOOR.)

22.   3   C
MCS of MIKE
sprawled on floor.

What in the name of .....

23.   2   D
2s HOLD PAT as
he comes round
table.

MIKE: It's me. I've got to see you.

PAT: What's wrong with you man?
Are you drunk or something?

24.   1   B
CU Back of MIKE'S
head. We see he
is injured. He
looks up to PAT.
TILT UP to MCU PAT
(POV shot)

PAT: Don't lie there. Get up and
tell me what you want.

25.   3   C
MLS PAT.
MIKE staggers
to his feet.

Is there something ailing you?

MIKE: They're out in the woods.
Can't you hear them?

26.   2   D
ARC LEFT as PAT
grabs MIKE'S arm
and seats him
in chair.

One of them hit me.

PAT: Are you badly hurt?
You look awful!

129

Production Paperwork

Most creative workers hate paperwork. It is time-consuming to prepare. We doubt its accuracy after changes have been introduced. It can be confining and restricting to freedom of thought.

In reality, paperwork is an unavoidable link in providing dependable, complete facilities and operation and in ensuring coherent, unified teamwork. The larger the organization, the greater the need. Production paperwork takes so many forms (literally!) ranging from contracts, requisitions, permits, expenses, etc., to those directly guiding the studio team. Each specialist job has its specific associated documents, to arrange facilities, materials, labour, transport. Some may be used to feed computers, some just to remind Joe of a 'phone call. But certain types of production paperwork are universal to all TV studio organization.

Scripts

The corrected draft script gives the story line/synopsis, dialogue, narration, basic scene-setting, action outline and stage directions. After working over, it becomes the *rehearsal script*. Here the page is split vertically. The existing script material is contained in the right-hand half, which is primarily concerned with audio information. As the director develops his picture treatment, this new camera information is typed in the blank left-hand section of the page. The combined script, now complete with all the production details the team needs to coordinate its shots, moves, cuing, timing, etc., has become the camera script.

A *semi-scripted* show usually follows a much simpler format. Basic camera shots are indicated, with anticipated action, any agreed dialogue such as introductory or concluding speech, with indications of questions, graphics inserts, etc.

Running order/show format

This list segments the production, showing the program items, the set areas (scenes) involved, video and audio facilities needed (lighting conditions), major running time, and intended segment durations, together with performers' names.

Camera cards/shot sheets/crib cards/shot list

The busy cameraman is too preoccupied to read a script. Instead, he has a series of cards clipped to his camera, giving him details for each of his shots. This includes the shot number, floor position (as marked on the camera plan), sometimes the lens angle, and a description of the shot (people involved, and their action) and camera movements, together with any additional instructions (e.g. 'Hold 2-shot as they go to the door'). It may contain, too, a rough sketch of the studio layout, showing respective positions of the cameras (1A, 1B, 1C, etc.).

130

Page	Scene	Shots	Cams/Booms		D/N	Cast
1	1. INT. WOODSHED	1 - 9	1A, 3A,	A1	DAY	Mike Jane
3	EXT. WOODSHED	10 - 12	2A,	F/P	DAY	Jane Jim
	RECORDING BREAK					
4	2. INT. SHOP	13 - 14	4A,	B1	DAY	George
6	3. EXT. WOODS	15	1B, 3B,	A2	DAY	Mike George
7	4. INT. SHOP	16 - 20	4A,	B1	DAY	George

CAMERA CARD

CAMERA ONE		THE OLD MILL HOUSE	STUDIO B

SHOT	POSN.	LENS ANGLE*	SET
2	A	24°	1. WOODSHED LS TABLE PAN MIKE L. to window.
5	(A)	35°	MS MIKE moves R. to stove JANE into shot L. Hold 2-shot as they X to wood-pile.

MOVE TO POSITION 'B' during Shot 6.

| 21 | B | 10° | BCU Door latch.
ZOOM OUT to MS as door opens. |
| 24 | (B) | 24° | CU back MIKE'S head.
As he looks up,
TILT UP to MCU of PAT
(POV shot) |

* OPTIONAL

131

Pre-studio Rehearsal

If a show has a *static* format (interviews, talks, quizzes, panels), rehearsal preliminaries may simply consist of the director discussing the production with the performers, so that they know what is expected of them. But where the production is mobile, complex, and contains interrelated action, where performance and timing are tightly controlled, pre-rehearsal before camera time is essential.

Preliminaries

It is self-evident that for any *dramatic* production, we need to arrange and practice the various moves, business, lines, etc., until all concerned have achieved interrelated performances. Rehearsals begin with a *briefing, read through or line rehearsal*, in which the director outlines his interpretation of the work, and the cast becomes familiar with reading lines together, and the required characterizations.

The equivalent stage for a *demonstration* program would be discussion and organization of the program format, the range and depth of the items and methods of presenting and demonstrating facts.

Pre-rehearsal/outside rehearsal

Studio time and space are usually at a premium. So, although it would be an advantage to be able to rehearse the entire show 'for real' in the setting to be used, this is generally impracticable. Instead, the performers have to be content with rehearsal under 'mock-up' conditions, in a convenient rehearsal hall or hired room.

Here the floor is taped or chalked with a full-size plan layout of the studio setting. Doors, windows, stairways etc. are outlined. Stock rehearsal furniture substitutes the actual items used in the studio, and major props such as a hatstand, phone or tableware are provided. The cast soon become accustomed to the scale and features of their surroundings, particularly where vertical poles, chairs or dummy doors mark the main architectural features.

The director arranges the positions, grouping and action to suit the production treatment he has in mind. He rehearses the production in sections: the cast, learning their lines, practicing their performances, moves and business, until the entire work runs smoothly, ready for its studio debut. The director scrutinizes rehearsals, standing in turn at his various planned camera positions, checking shots through a viewfinder, adjusting details as necessary.

Finally, a few days before the production is due in the studio, the specialists who were at the production planning meeting watch a *technical run-through*, checking and anticipating problems for cameras, lighting, sound, etc. This is the version from which the lighting plot and facilities are finalized.

132

Pre-studio rehearsal hints – initial blocking

The preliminary read-through will only give the roughest estimate of timing. But, after allowances have been made for typical business, action, recorded inserts, etc., a probable duration should emerge.

- Anticipate potential script cuts if overrun is evident.

- Ensure as early as possible that the performers have a clear idea of the program format, their part in it, and perhaps their interrelationship with others' contributions.

- Make sure that performers have a good notion of the setting (using sketches, models, plans), what it represents, where things are in it.

- Provide reasonable substitutes, where real props are not available.

- Where specific apparatus is involved, only the actual item to be used in the studio may suffice. (Where unfamiliar attire is eventually to be worn – e.g. sword, hoop-skirt, cloak – a rehearsal version is preferable to dummy motions.)

- Maintain a firm attitude towards punctuality, inattention and background chatter during rehearsals, to avoid needless time wastage and frustrations.

- Be careful that actors' positions are consistent and meaningful (i.e. they do not stand 'on' a wall), or shot arrangements become meaningless.

- Use a portable viewfinder to arrange shots. Even a card cut-out frame or a hand-formed frame is better than unaided guesses.

- Avoid excessive revisions of action, grouping, line-cuts, etc. Wrong versions get remembered, new ones forgotten.

- Always think in terms of *shots*, not of theatrical-styled groupings, entrances, exits, business. Start with clear ideas *at script stage* about what you want the camera to show, rather than arrange 'nice groups' and try to get 'good shots' during rehearsal.

- There is a tendency when setting up shots in a rehearsal hall to overlook the scenic background that will actually be present in the studio. Check shots with the set designer's plans and elevations.

- Performers should have a good idea of the shots you are taking – whether, for instance, they are in a revealing closeup, where even slight movement counts, or whether they are out of picture.

- Particularly when taking close shots, always consider depth-of-field limitations. Deep shots (with close and distant people framed together) may not be sharp overall on camera.

- Think in terms of practical studio mechanics. Rapid repositioning while looking through a viewfinder may be physically impossible with an actual camera.

- Try to bear sound and lighting problems in mind when arranging action and positions. For example, where individuals spaced widely apart talk consecutively, the sound boom may need time to swing, or have to be supplemented.

Studio Rehearsals

Directors work in several quite different ways, ranging from straight-through continuous shooting to piecemeal approaches.

Rehearsal begins – blocking

Some directors begin studio rehearsals with a *dry run (walkthrough)*, in which the studio crew watch a performance (without cameras) as they learn of the production format and treatment. (Remember, only key members of the team have attended planning and rehearsals.)

For most directors, though, rehearsals begin with *camera blocking (first run, stopping run, stagger through)*. A few prefer to work beside a mobile picture monitor on the studio floor, calling shots, checking and altering where necessary, until each section is complete. They then watch it as a continuous run, from the production control room. Most directors, however, remain in the production control room throughout, only 'going to the floor' (i.e. the studio action area) when personal, on-the-spot discussion is unavoidable. Otherwise, all communication to the crew is through the communal intercom system, while instructions to the talent pass through the floor manager.

In the *production control room*, the director (aided by an assistant) is doing several things simultaneously:

● Keeping a watchful eye on the *master (line/transmission) monitor* showing the 'on-air' pictures.

● Checking the shots displayed on the various *preview (channel) monitors*, and guiding cameras' shots.

● Sorting out any snags and snarl-ups (e.g. when a camera cannot get a shot, deciding on an alternative).

● Watching the talent, and assessing performance, delivery, action. Suggesting changes where necessary.

● Evaluating the program sound, scenic, lighting, makeup, costume/wardrobe treatments. Passing any observations on to the specialists concerned.

● Giving standby warnings to contributory channels (film, videotape) before cuing them to begin running.

● Cuing individual performance/action to start or stop.

● Cuing picture transitions (perhaps operating the switcher); cuing sound effects and music; cuing lighting changes, etc.

● Noting timings and durations of items (overrunning or underrunning allotted time?).

● Judging the effectiveness of the production.

(The producer, whose principal role has been to set up and mastermind the business and economic aspects of the production, may provide the director with critical comment and advice.)

Some directors rehearse and correct a scene or section at a time; while others cover an entire sequence or an act before correcting. Some prefer a *stop-start* method, picking up again before each error point. Others aim at a run that is as uninterrupted as possible.

Final stages

A *continuous run-through* is a 'polishing' rehearsal, giving a better idea of shot effectiveness, continuity, pace, timing, operational problems, etc. Only when it is unavoidable does one stop to remedy shortcomings. But the *dress-run* aims at an on-air performance, without any unscheduled stops, or errors.

Effective studio rehearsal

- Examine each shot. Modify it if necessary to improve positions, action, movement, composition.

- Consider *shot continuity*. Alterations may affect earlier shots, too. Remember, the crew and performers are *memorizing*. Their aids are the paperwork (script, camera cards, cue sheets) and your intercom reminders/instructions.

- Don't be vague. Make sure that everyone knows what you are seeking to do. Do not try to correct errors by unexplained instructions (e.g. 'Move it left a bit'). Indicate briefly *why* a shot is not working. Explain what it should be.

- Avoid too many changes and revisions or there will be hesitations and mistakes.

- Even in the first rehearsal, important *operational and performance errors*, misjudgements and inaccuracies should be checked directly they occur (e.g. camera in shot, shooting off, late cue, wrong lines, wrong shot, wrong mike). But avoid an over-interrupted rehearsal, or there will be poor continuity between shots.

- If a cameraman offers alternative shots, for example to overcome a problem, indicate if you accept it or disagree, and why.

- At the end of each scene or sequence, ask if there are any problems, and whether anyone wants to do that section again (cameras chalk their positions on floor).

- Various staging and lighting defects are unavoidable in early rehearsal. Certain details (set-dressing, light effects) take time to complete. Some aspects need to be seen on camera before they can be corrected, such as overbright lights or lens flares. Shot readjustments during camera rehearsal often necessitate lighting alterations.

- Never repeat a section (in rehearsal or recording) without saying whether it is to be *changed* (e.g. move faster next time), or is to correct an *error* (e.g. late cue), or to *polish* the performance/operations and let it flow more smoothly.

- Ensure that everyone knows when shots have been deleted, or new shots added (i.e. Shot 2A, 2B, 2C).

- At the end of each rehearsal, check timings, and give notes to performers/ cast and crew on any errors to be corrected, changes needed, problems to be solved. Check whether they have difficulties that need your aid.

- At least one complete, uninterrupted rehearsal is essential for reliable transmission

Rehearse/record

Here, individual shots or sequences are camera-rehearsed, then immediately recorded. This technique often uses only one TV camera, and provides great flexibility; particularly for directors unable to plan or organize multi-camera treatment. Drawbacks include the slow progress, considerable post-production editing, and continuity problems, compared with continuous-shooting methods.

135

The Floor Manager

The *floor manager (FM)* is the director's contact on the studio floor. He/she often joins the production when it reaches the studio. For larger shows, the FM may be involved from its earliest stages.

Rehearsal preparations
While the studio prepares for rehearsal (erecting/dressing sets, positioning lamps, cameras, sound equipment, etc.), the FM checks all non-technical aspects of the show.
- Will the various jobs be completed before scheduled rehearsal?
- Are there any problems (e.g. doors that stick)?
- Have *action props*, demonstration apparatus etc. arrived? Do they work?
- Have graphics, title cards etc. arrived?
- Are fire/safety regulations being complied with?
- Have performers arrived and been accommodated? Do they know where to go, when they are wanted, etc.?

The *director's assistant* gives out scripts to the studio crew, together with camera cards, running orders, etc., and checks the accuracy of all *titling* (cast lists, etc.).

Rehearsals begin
The studio crew (including cameras, sound) hear the director's *production intercom (talkback)* instructions over their headsets (earphones, earpieces) – unheard by the studio mikes or the performers. The FM may have a mini radio transmitter/receiver, or a long lead plugged into the intercom circuit.
- During rehearsals, the FM guides and cues performers, smoothing difficulties, and diplomatically relaying the director's messages.
- Only the FM will normally stop the rehearsal (on the director's behalf), to rearrange action or grouping, improve furniture positions, re-run action.
- The FM maintains general studio discipline (i.e. checks unnecessary noise).
- The FM investigates any disruptions or delays.
- The FM may speak to the director over radio intercom (reverse talkback), or one of the studio mikes. Often a hand gesture in front of a preview camera will suffice! Where the director needs to be shown a problem situation (e.g. an obstacle preventing a camera move), another camera may turn to reveal the difficulty.
- The FM announces all studio breaks, and recommencing times.
- At the end of a rehearsal, the FM checks the 'turn round'; i.e. ensures that scenes are readied for next time (e.g. a vase broken during action replaced).

Videotaping
- To begin *recording*, the FM readies the studio crew, counts down to the start, and hand cues action to begin. (During performance, the FM cues people when to enter, move, start a process, and when to stop.)
- At the end of recording, the FM holds the studio while the videotape is checked, then announces and prepares for any retakes.
- Finally, the FM releases the studio, talent disperses, sets and lighting are dismantled, equipment is stored. He/she checks out any special items (e.g. jewelry) to be collected, and logs a report.

136

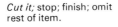

Stand by; go ahead.

Cut it; stop; finish; omit rest of item.

You are cleared; You are now off camera and can move, or stop action.

Volume up; louder.

Volume down; quiter (sometimes precede by "Quiet" signal).

Quiet; stop applause.

Tighten-up; Get closer together.

Open-up; Move further apart.

Come nearer; come downstage.

Go further away; go upstage.

You're on that camera, play to that camera; (Sometimes preceded by "Turning actor's head" gesture.)

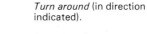

Play to the light indicated; (When actors are shadowing, point to light source and to area of face shadowed.)

Turn around (in direction indicated).

Speed up; faster pace; quicker tempo. (Movement's speed shows amount of increase).

Slow down; slower pace; stretch it out. (Indicated by slow "stretching" gesture).

O.K.; you're all right now; it's O.K. (Confirmation signal.)

We're/you're on time.

Are we on time? How is time going?

You have . . . time left (Illustrated—2 mins. and $\frac{1}{2}$ min).

Wind-up now.

To audience; *you can applaud now.* (May be followed by "Louder" signal).

Stop; (For applause, widespread action, etc.).

137

Guiding the Crew

Remote from the studio, the director must convey his ideas quickly and precisely.

Intercom

Sitting in the production control room remote from the studio, the director relies on the communal *intercom system (production talkback)* to coordinate operations, and convey his/her ideas quickly and precisely to the rest of the production team. There may also be *private lines* allowing the director to talk to individual cameras (camera talkback). During rehearsals, the crew usually speaks to the director over the studio mikes.

Attitude to the crew

The inexperienced director frequently has the urge to dash down to the studio floor to explain directly what he wants to do. Good TV direction does not work that way. It wastes rehearsal time, and while it helps individuals such as a cameraman, it often leaves others uninformed of changes now necessary (lighting or sound). The director must have a clear idea of what he wants. The crew may know little or nothing of his intentions, and they have relatively little time to find out what is expected of them, and to practice and coordinate their respective contributions.

Be patient! The dictatorial director is a pain in the neck – especially when he is wrong! But the undecided bumblings of the director who has not thought out his show, and relies on the crew to carry him, are no better. If an operation is not right, or has not been understood, find out if there is a problem. Listen to suggestions, and accept or reject them in firm, but friendly terms.

Always help the crew by warning them of action, particularly in early rehearsals. A quick guide, such as 'He's going to get up here' (prepare for a rise), smooths operations considerably. Let everyone know immediately about any extra shots or cuts.

General points

The preview monitors are your eyes. Watching them carefully, you can anticipate trouble, seeing that a boom will be in shot when you cut, that a shot is wrong. Corrections made on preview will prevent errors being seen on the transmission (main) channel.

End-of-rehearsal notes are either *instructive*, such as 'Zoom in faster on Shot 9', or *suggestions* like 'Will it help Camera 2 on Shot 25 if the girl pauses before moving?'. Make it clear when a rehearsal or taping session is over, and retakes complete. Never fail to thank the crew – particularly individuals who have done outstanding work.

138

Typical shot calls by the director's assistant

During rehearsal and transmission, the director's assistant continually passes information over the intercom, to guide continuity, prepare sources, and aid timing. Let us 'listen' to part of a typical, well-organized production.

CALLS	MEANING
On Shot 291 . . . 2 next	Shot 291 is 'on the air'. Stand by Camera 2.
Stand by film (or TK, i.e. telecine) Shot 292 . . . 3 next	Preparing film channel for cue.
On 3 . . . Film (or TK) next	On Camera 3. Film ready for cue.
Run film (or TK) . . . Counting down, 8–7–6–5–4–2–1–zero	Start cue to film, film-leader running, counting down to start.
On film for 3 minutes, 17 seconds	
One minute left on film. Out words '. . . and so to bed'. Coming to Shot 293, on Cam. 3.	End warning for film. Stand by for next shot.
30 seconds . . . 20–10–5–4–3–2–1–0	Counting back to the studio.
Shot 293 on 3	On Camera 3.
Shots 294, 295 are *out*	Warning reminder of shots cut from scripted version.
Next is 296 on 1 . . . steady 1	Stand by Cam. 1 (was not steady on his shot).
Shot 296 on 1 . . . 3 next	On Cam. 1. Stand by Cam. 3.
Extra shots 297 A and B	Warning reminder of shots added to scripted version.
Shot 297 on 3 . . . 297A on 2 next.	On Cam. 3. Stand by Cam. 2.
Shot 297A on 2 . . .	On Cam. 2.
Next 297B on 3	Stand by Cam. 3.
Shot 297B on 3. Stand by music and CG (character generator)	On Cam. 3. Stand by to audio tape and end titles.
Go music. Go credits	Cue to start audio taped music, and operate rolling end titles on character generator.
Stand by for retakes	Studio held while sections requiring re-recording selected.
We have a clear.	Videorecording checked and OK.

139

Production Timing

While a *closed-circuit* program needs only approximate timing, a *live production* fitting into a time-slot must often be accurate to a few seconds. Overruns can result in the end of the show being cut off (e.g. by commercial breaks), or cause scheduling problems. Inaccurate timing can completely abort any *composite production* in which various contributors 'opt in' or 'opt out' (temporarily join and leave) the main presentation, to insert their own material – e.g. weather, or news items.

Live productions
Videotape can always be edited to a suitable length, but 'live' or 'live-on-tape' presentations lack this flexibility. Time must be watched continually. In an unscripted discussion, an early subject could easily outstay its welcome, so that an important later one had to be curtailed owing to time shortage.

To ensure controlled timing, a good chairperson/anchor continually evaluates the situation, to ensure that agreed subjects are covered in allocated time periods. Where an item 'spreads' but is proving particularly productive, an editorial decision may deliberately restrict or drop others. If, despite careful timing, an item cannot be rounded off in the time available, it is often better to indicate that with an apology, rather than struggle to complete it.

Hints on timing
Scripts can be roughly timed by reading them aloud, and allowing for mute action, business or inserts. Many scripts run for around a minute a page. At any pre-studio rehearsal, time scene-by-scene, or section-by-section. Devise a *timed running order* showing the duration of each item (estimated, permitted, or actual), and indicate where adjustments are desirable.

Although live sequences can inadvertently run short (speed up) or spread, pre-recorded *inserts* are always of a known duration. Recorded sections offer little time flexibility (particularly when accompanied by a recorded commentary or dialogue), and can only be shortened – if at all – during transmission, by omitting the start or end.

Check all *recorded inserts* for their exact duration, and note their *out cues* (last words required). When cuing into the middle of material (e.g. excerpt from a speech) *in cues* may be needed, i.e. the first words to be heard. Wherever possible, the tops and tails of inserts should contain no speech or strong action.

To ensure that recorded music ends precisely at program fade out, time the music beforehand from a recognizable script point to its conclusion, e.g. 2 min 25 sec. On transmission, start the music (faded down) 2 min 25 sec before *program out-time*, and fade it in when convenient.

Methods of timing
Different methods of timing can be adopted according to the demands of the occasion.

Rehearsal timing
When rehearsal is halted for any reason, note the stopwatch time at that moment. When rehearsal recommences, go back to a point *before* the fault. Continue the overall duration check when the *fault-point* is reached.

Forward timing (front timing)
Duration timing (estimated and real) as the show proceeds.

Items (desired durations)	Running Stop Watch reads (from prog. start)	Clock Start Time	Clock End Time	Item Running Times (Actual duration)
Introduction 30″	30″	19.15.00	19.15.30	30″
Item A 10′	10′30″	19.15.30	19.25.30	10′
Item B 8′	18′30″	19.25.30	19.33.30	8′

Back timing
A *'remaining time'* measurement, showing the amount of time before the program ends.

Item Duration	Clock Time (Item Starts)	Remaining Time
1′	20.23.00	2′0″
Item Y 30″	20.24.00	1′0″
Item Z 30″	20.24.30	0.30″
End Titles Out Time	20.25.00	0.00″

Visual Padding

Although you can occasionally dispense with sound, blank screens are an anathema! Yet many subjects don't really have a strong *visual* element. Consider, for instance, discussions or musical performances. We are really concerned with what we are *listening to*; not what people look like. Speakers' expressions, instrument fingering etc. do not really have anything to do with the intrinsic *purpose* of the occasion (i.e. argument, debate, music). They may even distract us!

The problem
There are a surprising number of situations where there are no 'appropriate' subjects to shoot. They do not exist, or it is not possible to shoot them for some reason. Let's look at some typical examples:
- *Appropriate visuals too costly.* Budget limitations; would involve distant travel; copyright problems.
- *Forthcoming events.* Future projects; not yet happened.
- *Concluded events.* The event is all over; no trace remains.
- *Inaccessible events.* Where video/filming is not permitted.
- *Impractical situations.* Too dangerous, unstable or confined to shoot.
- *Historical events.* Before photography existed, or unphotographed.
- *Imaginary events.* Fantasy, hypothetical subjects.
- *Abstract subjects.* Philosophical; spiritual; social concepts (e.g. 'beauty').
- *General, non-specific subjects.* Weather; transport; humanity (e.g. 'mankind').

Solutions
A regular solution is to show someone standing at the scene, *telling* us about what we cannot *see*. It adds nothing, except a pseudo-authenticity. Talking heads are economical, but seldom compulsive viewing!

Instead you can get round the difficulty in other ways; usually by 'visual padding' ('wallpaper shots'):
- Show photographs, artists' sketches, library (stock) film, book/newspaper illustrations, even computer graphics, etc.
- When speaking of a *future* event, such as celebration days, or annual processions, you may be able to use material from *a previous occasion*, to suggest the atmosphere, or show its general form.
- Sometimes you can show a *substitute* subject; not the boat that sank, but one like it.
- *Associated subjects* are a useful ploy for 'visual padding'. When covering the childhood of a long-dead composer, for example, shots of his birthplace, or stock shots of the town, or even just a map.
- The same visual padding shot may be used for several different topics; e.g. a picture of 'wind-blown crops' to suggest 'Plenty', 'Trade', 'Agriculture', 'Insect pests', 'Prosperity', etc.
- *Abstract subjects* can be pressed into service on almost any occasion! Atmospheric shots of rippling water, shadows, light reflections, into-sun flares, defocused images – have their regular use!

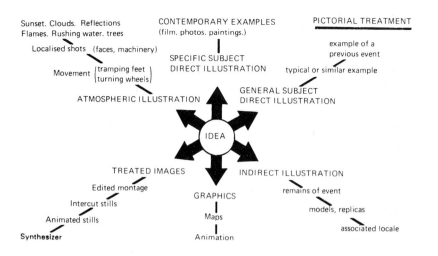

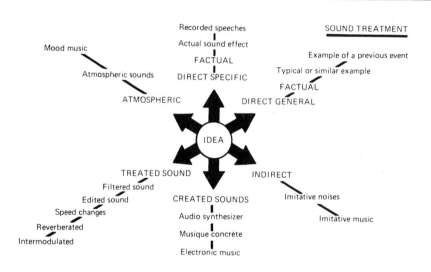

Methods of subject illustration

The most obvious way to depict a subject is to see it and to hear it directly.
Sometimes this is not possible. Sometimes a more imaginative, intriguing
approach is needed. There may be various solutions to the problem of presenting
attractive, appealing treatments in sound and picture.

143

How to Direct Audience Attention

There are certain dictums in shot organization. Every shot should have a purpose, however broad. It usually has a particular center of interest. It will normally continue a foregoing theme or argument, until we want to change to a new one. If we wish to convey specific ideas, we must discourage random thought-wandering. In an advertisement for floor polish, we do not want people distracted by costume, decor, and similar side issues. How do we achieve this?

Methods of directing attention

Fundamentally, we can cause the subject to *attract the eye*, or ensure that other aspects *do not* – i.e. form a *neutral* accompaniment.

We can direct attention to particular features in various ways.
- *Exclusion.* Take close shots. Avoid unwanted subjects. Simplify backgrounds.
- *Visual direction.* Pointing with a finger, pointer, inserted arrow or circle.
- *Aural indication.* A speaker draws attention to particular items/features.
- *Lighting treatment.* Localized lighting; other subjects half-lit.
- *Composition.* Using convergent line or pattern, balance, prominence through scale.
- *Color.* Using prominent hues against neutral or pastel hues. Using vibrant and discordant colors.
- *Camerawork.* By differential focusing, perspective, viewpoint, camera movement.
- *Subject movement.* Movement attracts, according to the speed, strength, direction of motion.

Look out for distractions

So you see, there are many varied ways in which we can attract and hold audience attention, but you can also see how easily attention can be distracted. If, for example, a person within a background group is dressed in startling contrast to others, or fluttering a fan, a director will often exclude them, rather than let attention be drawn away from the main foreground subject.

Varying concentration

You should aim to vary the audience's concentration pattern to suit the program material. Some shots say, 'I particularly want you to note this point', while others encourage the viewers to look around or reflect a little, or may provide a shot of a general nature that enables them to concentrate on the audio instead (i.e. listening to commentary, dialogue, music). But do not attempt to sustain concentration for too long, or interest will fall, and minds wander.

Exclusion
By keeping other items out of shot, attention can be concentrated on the main subject.

Visual direction
Where rapid, unambiguous identification is essential, an indicator or marker (circle, arrow) is invaluable.

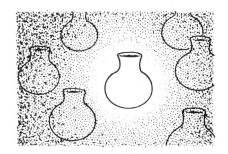

Isolation by lighting
Lighting can be arranged to isolate the required subject.

Composition
Here the eye is drawn to the main subject. The others serve as a visual support.

145

Creating and Controlling Interest

Audience interest is one of our primary concerns when creating a production. Without it, our show is a dead duck! Even a captive classroom audience cannot be *made* to pay attention, only encouraged!

Interesting pictures
Certain kinds of pictures have a higher associated interest than others. For instance, a shot with strongly contrasted tones is more arresting than the subtle half-tones of a high-key picture. A picture showing clear detail encourages scrutiny, while a soft-focused version does not. Similarly, strong dynamic composition draws the eye, while weak diverse lines do not.

Progressive build-up
Intrigue your audience, but try not to puzzle or frustrate in the process. Do not put all your goods in the store window at once! Conversely, don't keep the audience waiting too long, or fail to deliver.

Information should be presented systematically, and consecutively. One idea should develop out of another. Disjointed, piecemeal facts lose their significance. If the production essentially comprises many isolated points, group them together in sections – even if their relationships are rather slight – and present them as a series of contained groups.

Avoid over-complexity, or an excess of information. Our audience needs time to examine and absorb facts. Too many facts just become an unheeded stream of words, heard but not understood.

If the shot is held for too short a time, it does not make its point. Retain it for too long, and interest inevitably fails. The optimum duration varies with the shot content, and the situation. Camera movement (or zoom) or a cut to a new viewpoint may need to be introduced to sustain interest.

Elaborate presentation
Thanks to a wide range of staging and electronic devices, considerable visual elaboration is possible – even on a small budget. Decorative effects, presentational gimmicks and unusual displays can certainly create interest. But all too often the viewer reacts to such ingenuity by becoming intrigued with the effect itself, rather than its purpose! One can become more preoccupied with a singer's surroundings than with her performance. One looks at the dramatic effects, and wonders how they did them. In such circumstances, elaboration can be self-defeating.

Composition
A unified composition attracts attention to a particular subject or area.

The picture may contain an assembly of items, but the eye may not be encouraged to any particular aspect of the shot.

Visibility is not everything
Although details cannot be seen clearly, audience interest is high. We are intrigued to know more.

Influencing Audience Attitude

The presentational style adopted for the production can have a considerable influence on the audience's attitude to it.

Program openings
Opening titles herald the intended character of the presentation. Rapid, brash animations invite the audience lightheartedly. Archaic script and earnest, regal music suggest historical occasions (real or fictional), to be taken seriously. The type face, its size, color, background, etc., create a foretaste of the program.

Staging complexity
Elaboration of decor, too, can influence how the viewer evaluates the production. Simplicity of presentation can appear clear-cut, direct, sophisticated – or sparse, frugal, uninteresting. Elaborate presentation can seem rich, interestingly complex, having great variety – or fussy, confusing, with individual features being lost.

Background associations
It is interesting to see how strongly the associations of a setting can influence the audience's attitude towards the subject. Where action is staged in a classroom, study or museum, overtones of scholarship give the subject authority. But if the subject is shown in a junkyard, it becomes correspondingly devalued. A coin looks more imposing displayed on velvet than heaped with others in a rusty tin box!

Prevailing key
In *high-key* pictures, light tones predominate, with few dark tones. The effect (whether achieved by staging tones or lighting treatment) embues a light, fresh, brittle atmosphere. *Low-key* pictures, on the other hand, have a sombre, serious dramatic connotation.

Subject importance
The subject can be made to appear important, trivial, large, small or dramatic, according to the way we shoot it. The camera height and viewpoint, speed of movement, transitions and cutting rate can all influence the audience's attitude towards the subject.

Further factors
Being so close to the presentation ourselves, we can easily overlook the effect of various factors. Whether a presenter appears casual, reverent, indifferent or enthusiastic can create an ambience for the entire show. The complexity of terms and speed of delivery can affect how easily a viewer follows the argument. Even background sounds can directly modify audience attitude.

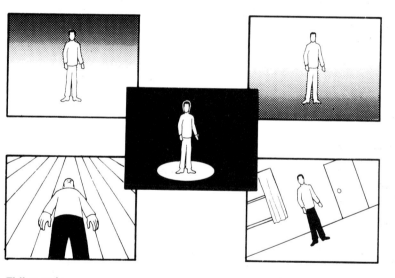

Titling style
The style of lettering should herald the style of the production. The type face proclaims: dignity, occasion, fun, ruggedness, period atmosphere, etc.

Subject presentation
The presentation can affect our attitude to the subject. The subject can be dominated, or given strength or instability.

149

Confusing or Frustrating Techniques

It's not difficult to confuse, frustrate or antagonize your audience!

The frustrated audience
Don't leave your audience feeling that they are *missing interesting subjects*. It's better to keep items out of shot than have the viewer tantalized at being unable to see them properly. Regular frustrations include:
- Subjects soft-focused, partly hidden (masked), or shadowed.
- Subjects that merge with the background.
- Shots too distant to see the subject properly.
- Titling or graphics that are not held for long enough for you to read.
- Occasions when book titles, or an interesting-looking notice in the background, are *nearly* sharp enough to read.
- Watching a cook, instead of what he is cooking.
- Situations that dwell on one feature for too long, when there are many others to be seen.
- Demonstrators preoccupied with putting on a performance, rather than getting on with the job.
- Occasions when the camera concentrates on a commentator, instead of showing us the interesting surroundings.

Promises, promises!
Don't seem to promise what you don't deliver! A long shot of an art gallery where we never see the exhibits close to is infuriating. When looking at interesting items, it is frustrating to be told that there's no time to see more — especially if the program continues with a trivial item.

Annoying attitudes
- The speaker who always 'sincerely' parrots the same old opening phrase; e.g. 'Hello and good evening'.
- The speaker who appears to be busy, and not ready for us; e.g. 'Hello. I'll be with you in just a moment.'
- An interviewer who is more preoccupied with notes than the guest.
- An interviewer who handles a guest's exhibits carelessly or casually.

Unseen happenings
It can be very frustrating when you know that there is interesting action nearby, but you can't hear or see it properly, because the camera is watching something else!

Wrong camera
- Performers who are cued wrongly, and have already started, or stand with 'egg on the face', wondering what to do.
- A cut to an unrelated subject or viewpoint.
- A new person speaks, but the camera remains on an irrelevant shot.
- We see just a glimpse of the actual subject, then someone *talks about it* instead of showing it!

Puzzling shots
- Don't leave the viewer wondering what he is supposed to be looking at.
- Avoid too many different things happening in the same shot (*split centers of attention*).

150

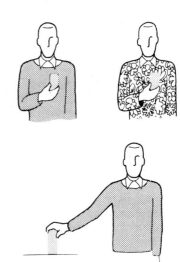

Background contrast
Hand-held items are often shot against an unsuitable background – a tone or hue that is too similar to the subject, or of confusing pattern. By holding it against a suitable background, visual clarity is improved.

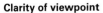

Clarity of viewpoint
Is the camera viewpoint the optimum for the particular aspects to be shown? Any of these *could* be appropriate. It depends on the point to be made.

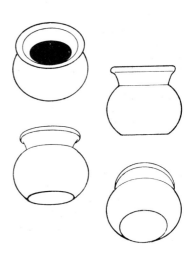

151

Stretching the Facilities

When you are shooting *'live' continuous action*, there will be times when you want to do just a little more than your facilities allow.

Even in a multi-camera setup, a fast-moving sequence can find the director taking shots quicker than the cameraman can set up new ones! And then there are occasions when there is insufficient time to move a camera to its new viewpoint, or obstructions such as floor cables impede a camera move. A live single camera setup can be very restrictive.

With a little ingenuity, you can improve such situations, and provide a rapid succession of different shots, despite restrictions.

Useful devices

• *Using inserts.* The simplest method of stretching facilities is to switch to a videotape or film insert, while repositioning the camera(s). As well as the more obvious kinds of insert, such as an illustrative sequence, you can introduce recorded *cutaway shots* of an audience, a *detail shot* showing closeup views of the subject, or even a *reaction shot (nod shot)* of the anchor person taped during rehearsal.

Similarly, you could cut to a *slide scanner* showing some appropriate subject, such as a map or a graphic. Even a brief animated graphic or decorative effect from a desktop video/computer may be sufficient to reposition the camera or change the shot.

• *Rapid intercutting.* If you are showing a series of items, and want to intercut between them quite quickly, arrange them in arcs at equal distances from the cameras, so that all they have to do is to pan between objects without moving position.

• *Turntable.* This is a simple yet effective way to present items. Place the subject in the centre of a revolving turntable, and you can show all sides of it, without having to laboriously arc the camera round it. Alternatively, you can use the turntable to present a series of small displays in quick succession.

• *Front-projected slides.* Project a photo-slide onto a screen, and the camera can take in the whole or part of the picture, or explore around the projected image. You can even insert this picture into another camera's shot as a chromakeyed background.

• *Mirror.* A carefully placed mirror allows you to pan the camera from one subject to another that is reflected in the mirror. The effect is a 'pushover wipe'.

• *Pull-out graphics.* Used since the earliest days, a grooved box holding a series of pull-out graphics (graphs, titling, mattes) still has its uses.

152

METHODS OF RAPID SHOT CHANGE

Quick pans
Rapid intercutting is possible, if cameras pan quickly between equidistant items.

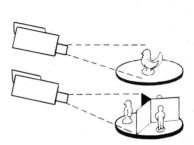

Turntables
Turntables enable various aspects to be seen easily, or to provide rapidly changed displays.

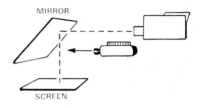

Front projected slides
A compact device for projecting and shooting slides uses a 45° mirror.

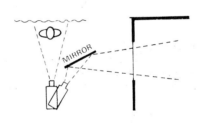

Instant repositioning
With a quick pan to a mirror, the camera is virtually repositioned to a new viewpoint.

Pull-out graphics
Using a series of pull-out graphics in a grooved box, rapid changes are possible.

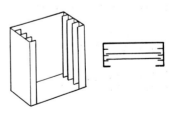

Economy Thinking

Effective presentation does not necessarily involve costly, elaborate methods. 'Economy', however, does not have to produce a frugal, spartan, cheap-looking product. It is an attitude of mind; using facilities effectively, imaginatively, ingeniously and to good effect.

'Economy thinking' is realizing that we need only to provide in the studio just what the camera is going to see (plus a little extra, perhaps, to avoid over-shooting). This necessitates careful planning. The skilled designer creates an *illusion* through ingenuity.

In a dramatic presentation, a single look or gesture can prove more telling than intricate production treatment. As a camera shoots through a foreground branch, we have the impression of a forest – without needing to plant entire trees! In 'economy thinking', we start with the *effect*, and devise the most economical method of obtaining it. There are times when *silence* can engender spine-chilling tension and others when a background of street noises or bird song gives a scene absolute conviction. There is no universal rule.

Economical staging

This is staging to stimulate the imagination. It may be based on *simple mechanics* (e.g. using a cyclorama and projected light patterns, or even a black background and isolated foreground furniture) or on *cost-saving constructional methods* (e.g. stock scenery, revamped sets) or *special effects* (e.g. chromakey, front or rear projection).

Sometimes an associative lighting effect alone (e.g. a projected window shadow, a spotlight, leaf-shadows) can convey a location or environment – especially when supported by allied background sounds.

Economy through camera treatment

Carefully thought-out camera treatment can save time and money, and simplify equipment needs.
- You can arrange action so that it *works to the camera*, e.g. a dancer runs from long shot to closeup, rather than having the camera itself dolly in rapidly. Camerawork is simpler. The camera will not be in the way of subsequent shots.
- Shooting via a mirror, the camera can turn in an instant from a *high shot*... tilting down to a level shot, without the need for a camera crane or special equipment.
- Reshoot a sequence from several different angles with a *single camera*, and the result appears to be a *multi-camera* treatment.

Graphics and titling

- Set the scene by shooting a still photograph (or projected slide) of the Eiffel Tower, backed with street noises and French music, and the simple brick wall in your studio appears located in Paris!
- Large display graphics are expensive. So instead, where possible,
  - use rear-project slides,
  - or use chromakey to insert close shots of smaller photographs.
- 'Improvized' titles look different. They are simple, yet attract the attention; e.g. titles chalked on a wall, or drawn in wet sand with a finger.

154

Effective frugality
With a minimum of scenery, the shot conveys a country scene; enhanced by sound effects of bird song and wind.

Partial set
Only part of the environment is needed – so only part is built.

Light patterns
Light patterns on the cyclorama provide a cheap, adaptable, decorative background to action.

155

Sound Ideas

Sound does not simply *accompany* pictures. It contributes subtly to their effectiveness. Through music or sound effects you can create illusion; suggesting a time or place, a situation. You can build up a mood, suggest foreboding, horror, comedy.

Depending on the accompanying sound, the same picture can convey entirely different meanings; e.g. a display of flowers, suggesting a ballroom, a wedding, a funeral.

You can devise an atmospheric sound picture for subjects where no sounds actually exist; e.g. sculpture, painting, architecture.

Where appropriate associated sounds were absent when shooting a scene (e.g. birdsong), you can add them later. You can even add sounds as an ironic *comment*; e.g. shots of a derelict factory, accompanied by sounds of busy manufacture.

The roles of sound

● To *explain* the picture; e.g. a falling guillotine blade, and the roaring crowd symbolizing 'the French Revolution'.
● To *interpret* the picture; e.g. uncertain music suggests that the man walking along the street is sleepy and confused.
● To *augment* the picture's meaning; e.g. a ship's cabin – sounds of fog horns tell us of local conditions.
● To *strengthen* the picture's impact; e.g. shots of a storm, accompanied by loud thunder.
● To *enrich* the picture's appeal; e.g. pictures of spring flowers, and pastoral music.

Interrelating picture and sound
We need to remember certain general principles when combining sound and picture:

● The scale and quality of sound and picture should match – e.g. reverberation should be appropriate for the surroundings shown.
● When visual action and sound are directly related, as in lip movements or hammering, they should be synchronous.
● Switching between pictures is best done to the beat of music, rather than against it; preferably at the end of a phrase. Continual cutting in time with music quickly becomes tedious and mannered.
● Sound can be used to create continuity (bridge) for a series of otherwise unrelated shots.
● Sound and pictures should normally begin and end together, particularly at the start and finish of a show. Fade out as a musical phrase ends . . . unless you are aiming at a feeling of indecision or suspense.
● Starting the next scene's sound before the present scene has finished may suggest continuity (but can also be confusing).

Using audio recordings
As well as providing background music and sound effects, audio recordings have other less obvious uses:

● As *voices off (VO)* – for people not seen on camera (outside the door; other end of phone conversation; being overheard).
● As *sound-over (SO, SOV)* – dialogue or commentary over mute shots. Sound effects for mute shots.
● As *sound inserts* – e.g. the telephone voice of an eye-witness over news item shots.
● As a *prerecorded substitute* during a live show – a person miming to an audio tape of their own singing, while moving around the setting.

156

SOUND BACKGROUNDS

MOOD MUSIC

SYNTHETIC SOUNDS

PERIOD MUSIC

ATMOSPHERIC EFFECTS

PASTORAL SOUNDS

MUSIC OF THE COUNTRY

Audio can complement the picture
Where the subject itself is mute, or has no directly associated sound that is appropriate, a contrived audio background can enhance the presentation. It can be imitative, reminiscent, environmental, associative, and so on.

157

Unorthodox Treatment

There are always occasions when you want to use some kind of unusual treatment: to give the situation a fresh look, to create shock, excitement or amusement, or simply to make it more interesting.

Camera treatment
Typical forms of visual treatment include:

- Pull focus (from one distance to another).
- Crash zoom. Zoom jumps.
- Overhead (through ceiling) shots.
- Low shots taken from ground level, or vertically upwards.
- Canted shots; tilting off horizontal to suggest instability.
- Vehicles racing towards the camera, apparently running over it. (Use an isolated camera, or shoot via a mirror.)
- Cameras clamped low on a traveling vehicle.
- Modified camera images, using diffusion disks, soft-edged filters, strong sky filters, star filters, multi-image filters.

Switcher treatment

- Superimposed images.
- Wipes.
- Outline generation (subject is converted to an outline).
- Silhouette generation (converting subject to a silhouette).

Electronic treatment
Images modified electronically, to produce:

- Exaggerated or diminished tonal values (gamma adjustment).
- Exaggerated or diminished color (adjust saturation).
- Color suppressed, or converted to, for example, sepia.
- Picture 'posterized' (reduced to just a few tonal steps).
- Picture (or part of it) broken up into small squares (mosaic).
- Electronically softened picture.
- Chromakey used to insert pattern or texture to subjects.
- Color changes (chosen color substituted with another).
- Multi-image generation.
- Picture speed changes, from fast motion to slow motion, reverse motion, repeat motion, time lapse, pixilation, freeze frames, etc.

Sound treatment
Audio, too, can be manipulated to produce many unusual effects:

- Quality changes (audio filtering; distortion).
- Reverberation (adjustable artificial reverberation devices).
- Pitch changes (from 'chipmunk' speech to slowed-down effects).
- Speed changes.
- Reversed sound.
- Repeated sounds (stutter effects).

Lighting treatment
A wide range of lighting equipment is available to produce unusual light effects:

- Flashing lights (e.g. 'chaser' lights, flashing patterns, lightning).
- Moving lights (e.g. mirror ball, moving pattern projectors, lasers).
- Light patterns (using 'gobo' stencils, slides, cast shadows).
- Color effects (color changes, color mixtures).

158

Overhead shot
An overhead view can reveal
decorative effect, grouping and
movement.

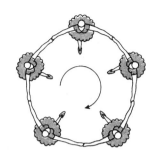

Alternatively, the overhead shot
can give the audience a dramatic
overall view, so that they can see
the intruder behind the door, and
the unsuspecting newcomer.

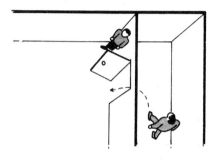

Ground shot
An extremely dramatic viewpoint
that can be achieved by shooting
into a low mirror or using a very
low camera mounting, or staging
the scene on an elevated area.

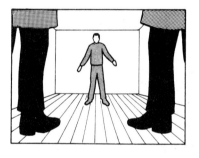

Canted shot
The canted (tilted) shot remains
one of the most effective ways of
conveying instability, fear,
madness, etc.

159

Continuity

Most people are familiar with the fundamental problem of *continuity* in film-making; e.g. someone who was out in a storm enters a room . . . and appears completely dry! Because sequences are shot in the most convenient order (which is usually different from the final edited running order), errors and incongruities can easily arise.

Regular continuity problems
- *Temporal discontinuity.* When the visual clues to the passing of time are inconsistent in successive shots; i.e. clock time, seasons, ageing.
- *Physical discontinuity.* Variation in appearance or physical state between shots; clothing, action, items being consumed or used; e.g. wearing a raincoat in one shot, but not the next.
- *Location discontinuity.* A person unexplainedly changes their location; e.g. we see them standing in one place . . . cut to a graphic . . . cut back to them, and they are now somewhere else.
- *Pictorial discontinuity.* Where there is supposed to be continuity, an exterior should not appear 'day' in one shot, and 'night' in the next. A series of shots should be reasonably matched in brightness, exposure, color quality.
- *Spatial discontinuity.* Loss of any sense of direction or location during intercutting; particularly where backgrounds are similar (e.g. in a forest). Has A nearly caught up with B or is he still some distance behind?
- *Attention discontinuity.* On switching, having to search around the new picture to find where the subject is.
- *Relationship discontinuity.* Mismatched cuts, causing the subject's position in the frame to change considerably on the cut, momentarily disrupting the picture flow (jump cuts, reverse cuts).

Deliberate discontinuity
We do not need to see every moment of an action sequence to follow what is going on. A car stops outside a house, and an instant later, we see the person entering a room. All the intermediate action is omitted, to quicken the pace. The TV/film audience has long since been accustomed to the conventions of *filmic time* in which the action jumps on in time, and *filmic space* intercutting action that is concurrent at different places.

Similarly, in a cooking demonstration, we realize that we are not seeing every moment of the process, and a mix/dissolve becomes a time transition between stages.

Cutaway shots are now so accepted as a way of introducing 'time jumps' or 'viewpoint jumps' that the audience is usually unaware of the subterfuge.

Broken continuity

When retaking action, avoid broken continuity due to articles having been consumed or repositioned throughout the original take. Action and positions should be matched.

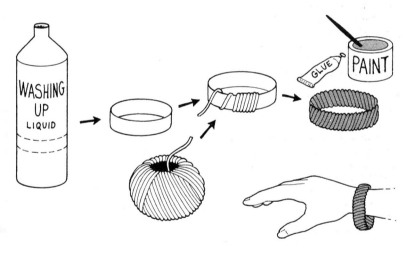

Deliberate discontinuity

The various stages of making a decorative bangle from a plastic bottle section wrapped with string. Showing isolated steps, saves the time and tedium of watching the entire process in continuity.

Using Titling

Every production uses displays of lettering in one form or another:
- Program title (the name of the show).
- Introductory credits (production principals, cast list).
- Identifying titles/subtitles (location, performer, subject).
- Time (showing clock time, time taken).
- Graphics (tables, lists, charts, etc.).
- End credits (production team, cast list).

Titling methods
Many titling methods are available today – from hand-lettering to rub-on transfers, from lettering kits to computerized titling software. Instead of *title cards* or *crawls/roller-captions* set up in front of cameras, or titles prepared on *photo-slides*, electronic systems are now increasingly used.

The *caption generator (CG)* allows typed lettering to be inserted directly into the video picture. You can adjust its size, shape, style, color; make it flash, flip, crawl (sideways), roll (vertically), animate . . . Titles can be stored and presented on cue. *Desktop video* using personal computers similarly offers titling facilities with a variety of fonts and backgrounds.

Titling design and presentation
As well as selecting an appropriate *style* for the show, it is important to avoid certain features:
- Keep lettering away from the edges of the frame.
- Don't overcrowd the screen with lettering. Too much becomes difficult to read.
- Don't present your information too fast for people to assimilate! (Read it out loud twice, before changing, to assist your slowest reader.) Very fast sequences look ridiculous.
- If you have a voiceover repeating displayed information, make sure that the spoken version corresponds!
- Lettering smaller than, for example, $\frac{1}{10}$ screen height is hard to discern.
- Leave a minimum space between title lines of about $\frac{1}{2}$ to $\frac{2}{3}$ the height of capital letters.
- Lettering formed from thin lines, hatching, thin stripes or elaborate structures will not reproduce well.
- Have a good tonal and color contrast between titling and background.
- Avoid strongly saturated colors that can dazzle or 'bleed' (especially red), or unpleasant color relationships (e.g. blue letters on a red background).
- Parts of titling may merge into a multi-tone/ multi-color background.

Electronic enhancement
You can improve the clarity and impact of titling electronically. The commonest device is the *border generator (edge keying, black edge)* which puts a black (or white) border around letters to emphasize them. Using this system, you can even insert white lettering into a white background (it puts a black outline round characters). Titling can be given a broad outline shadow around part or all of the characters (*drop shadow*). Black or white titling and backgrounds can be colored by keying in (matting) electronically generated color from a *color synthesizer*.

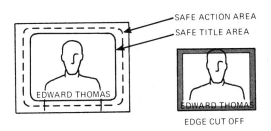

SAFE ACTION AREA

SAFE TITLE AREA

EDGE CUT OFF

Titling safe area

To avoid parts of titling being lost beyond the edge of the average TV screen, make sure that it falls within the safe title-area. (Action should be kept within the safe action-area limits.)

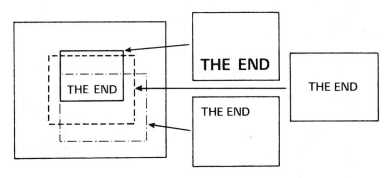

Titling card size

If a title is set within a fairly large black background, the camera can frame it in various ways.

Title positions

Titling can be localized to prevent it obscuring the subject, or for visual variety.

163

Using Graphics

The term *graphics* (*captions*) covers all the two-dimensional visuals used in the production – diagrams, charts, maps, graphs, titling, etc.

Forms of graphics
Graphics can range from scribbled roughs to immaculate pseudo-three-dimensional art. Graphics can be presented as cards/boards set up in front of a camera or within a setting. Photo-slides of graphics can be front or rear projected, or scanned by a slide-projector. Static or animated graphics can be created electronically (*computer graphics, desktop video*). Solid three-dimensional graphical models are occasionally used.

Simple graphics
The simplest, most versatile form of graphic is card-mounted artwork supported in front of a camera. You can shoot the entire graphic, select various parts of it, or explore it with the camera. You can fill the TV screen, or *inset (insert)* it as a small segment of the shot. Using chromakey, the graphic can become the entire background of the shot.

There are various simple tricks, such as placing a black card over a list of names, and progressively revealing them, or using the switcher to *wipe* names in/out. If you videotape a graph in a series of very brief takes, adjusting it or adding details between each, it will appear animated when the tape is run. Simple animation may just involve interswitching; e.g. between 'hand-up' and 'hand-down' versions.

Care with camera graphics
• Wherever possible, arrange graphics in 4 wide by 3 high overall proportions. Otherwise the camera will overshoot or miss parts of the graphic. (To prevent this, use a large black backing card.)
• Keep important details away from the edge of the frame, to avoid cut-off.
• For best results, limit detail and information. Small detail, close fine lines etc., will not reproduce well.
• The ideal graphic's surface is matte, flat, with no buckling, curling, blistering, wrinkles.
• When shooting camera graphics, avoid fast intercutting between a series of rapid changed cards. It only requires one false change, a wobble or misalignment, to wreck the sequence.
• It's easier and more reliable to *zoom* on a graphic card (remember to *prefocus*), than to *dolly (track)* in/out (problems in following focus).
• Always shoot a graphic *head-on* to avoid distortion.
• Surface light reflections or glare may be remedied by slightly angling the graphic.

Computer graphics
Depending on software and design, computers can produce a variety of effects, such as line drawing, 'watercolor', 'poster', 'oils' and textured 'brushes' in several styles. You can introduce logos, symbols, and prearranged effects from library files. 'Grab' a video still or a photo shot, and you can treat it in many ways: adding, altering or removing details; modifying color and textures.

Typical camera graphics sizes (4 units across, by 3 units down)

cm	in	
30.5 × 23	12 × 9	Smallest for convenient handling
40 × 30	16 × 12	
61 × 46	24 × 18	Larger sizes are unwieldy

Thickness of support card (minimum) 2 mm ($^{1}/_{16}$″)

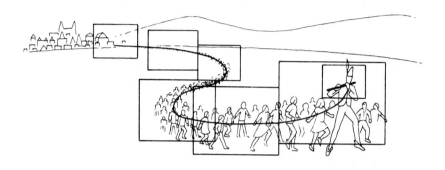

Exploring graphics
By exploring a detailed graphic with the camera, a story can be told while providing continual visual change.

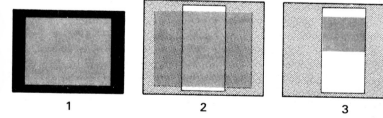

| 1 | 2 | 3 |

Aspect ratio
1. Only a graphic in 4 by 3 proportions will fit the TV frame. graphic can be shot as a whole but with black side borders. selected areas.

2. A tall narrow 3. It can be shot in

Using Film

Many program packages are still shot entirely on film for TV transmission; but film is being used less and less in the actual television production process.

Directing techniques
Film is invariably shot with a single camera, one setup at a time. Because results can only be confirmed after processing, filming relies on careful measurements (exposure and color temperature) and subsequent grading by film labs. Multi-takes and repeated action provide greater editing flexibility. (Only around 1/10 to 1/20 of the material shot is actually used – a 10:1–20:1 shooting ratio.)

The optical viewfinder of some film cameras includes a tiny video camera, which allows shots to be checked on a nearby picture monitor. But the director is always very dependent on the cameraman for the final film quality.

All editing decisions and selections are made after shooting is over, in collaboration with the film editor. General speaking, filmed sequences have briefer shots (and hence a faster pace), with more frequent change of viewpoint or location, than video productions.

Televising film
Film is converted into the television image either by special *telecine* scanning equipment, or a *film chain (film island)* housing a film projector shot by a video camera.

A 'standard' *leader* is usually attached to the beginning ('head') of a film insert, containing numbered frames counting down at one-second intervals. This allows its start to be cued accurately. (While some equipment has 'instant start', most takes several seconds to get up to speed and stabilize sound.)

When there are several inserts (film clips) on a roll of film, they will usually have individual leaders. but if you are cutting frequently to and from a series of inserts, it may be preferable to insert black leader (*blanking*) of suitable durations between them, and leave the equipment running. Film rewind time may have to be allowed for during rehearsal, particularly if the film sound is recorded on a separate magnetic track (*sep. mag.*).

Library shots
Film libraries have extensive collections of *library* or *stock* shots, which can be integrated into a production. These cover virtually all subjects: location shots, news events, personalities, special effects, industrial processes, etc. Apart from the fact that it would often be quite impracticable to shoot or restage new material, these library shots provide very convenient, economic picture sources.

There are disadvantages to using library material. Certain often-used shots can become too familiar to the audience. Picture quality is very variable (sometimes black and white), and may not match unobtrusively with video shots.

Where library prints are mute (no sound) or their sound is unsuitable, you can add your own sound effects/music.

The basics of film making

Shooting
- *Pictures* are shot by a single film camera, in separate setups. Action is repeated/varied to improve the 'take', or assist editing continuity. (Maximum shooting time typically 10 min.)
- Identifying *clapper board* is held in front of camera at start of each take; or shown inverted at the end.
- While shooting the picture, *sound* is usually recorded on separate ¼-in magnetic tape audio recorder. Electronic interlock ensures accurate synchronism between film camera and audio recorder. (Some systems now use *time code* methods of ident. and syncing.)
- Details of all takes *logged* for future reference.

Processing
- 'Takes' are processed, to produce a *master negative* (all tones/hues reversed). An uncorrected positive print of negatives is made from this – in B & W for economy. These 'rushes' ('dailies') are used to check/review the shots (action, framing, focus, etc.).

Editing
These rough prints are then used for the editing process: spliced together in potential order, matching sequences so that action *appears* continuous. The resulting *work print* or *rough cut* is checked/revised, and each join marked to show transition required. This *cutting copy* or *fine cut* is sent to *film laboratories ('labs')*.

Audio
Dub transfer. The original ¼-in audio tape is transferred selectively onto fully coated sprocketed magnetic film, to correspond with the 'cutting copy'.
  This track (usually dialogue) is then exactly synchronized to the picture.
- Various additional sound tracks for sound effects, music, commentary etc. are individually prepared and assembled.
- The specialist *dubbing mixer* plays all tracks, introducing and blending them at appropriate moments in the film (at the same time adjusting audio quality/reverberation where necessary). Result is a single mixed soundtrack (mono or stereo) that exactly matches the edited film.
- Where necessary, the original film sound is replaced or treated. Unsatisfactory dialogue may be substituted (*dubbing, post-syncing, looping*).

Processing
- *Grading, timing, cinex strips.* The labs provide short test strip prints of each scene, showing variations/corrections of exposure and color balance. The versions approved later guide the lab's processing adjustments (timing/grading).
- Exactly following the editor's 'cutting copy/fine cut', labs cut and assemble the precious original master negative shot by the camera – using its edge numbers (or time code) as a guide.
  A special *optical printer* provides transitions and effects, corresponding with the editor's joint markings.
- The 'show print' made from this final negative may be a *combined print* – optical or magnetic soundtrack alongside the picture; or *double-headed* – soundtrack on *separate magnetic film* run synchronously in telecine.
- Film *negative* can be transmitted (electronically reversed) to save time and costs.

167

Using Videotape

Videotape recording facilities have transformed television production.

Principles
- *Picture.* All types of VCR/VTR use a *helical scan* method of recording the color picture. However, their technicalities vary, and the present 15 or so *different* formats are incompatible, and so will only handle tapes recorded on their own particular system.
- *Audio.* All systems record the *sound* simultaneously on the tape (in mono or stereo). Some have a soundtrack along the tape edge; others also use special 'depth multiplex' Hi-Fi audio tracks, recorded along with the video tracks.

Editing the videotape
When *film* is edited, sections are selected, cut out and spliced together into the required order. Videotape must *not* be cut. It would not only permanently damage the tape, but would upset picture and sound at that point.

Instead, videotape is edited by *re-recording* chosen sections from the original *1st generation* master tape. There are two main disadvantages to this copying or 'dubbing' process. With most videorecording formats (except digital systems), picture and sound quality deteriorate a little in the copy (*2nd generation*). If you then make a copy of that copy (*3rd generation*), degrading becomes more noticeable (picture noise, smearing, lower color fidelity, etc.) and so on. Secondly, copying involves changing cassettes, and shuttling to and fro to selected sections; a time consuming process.

The editing process
Although you can *edit in camera* by starting/stopping recording *while shooting*, it is preferable to simply record sequences, and leave all editing until later.

There are two basic methods of editing, each with advantages and drawbacks:
- In *assemble (assembly)* editing, you add new material *on the end* of the previous sequence.
- In *insert* editing, you add new material *within* an existing recorded sequence.

Off-line editing. The first stage in VT editing is to take a copy of the original videotape which includes a *timecode* display at the bottom of the picture showing when each moment was recorded. Running this tape, the director or editor notes the points at which required sections begin and end. This *edit decision list* is used to guide the actual editing mechanics.

On-line editing. The source tapes are loaded on replay VCRs/VTRs, which are connected to an *edit controller*. Depending on its design, this device, guided by the edit decision list, rolls the machines to the selected sections, and copies them in order (with the appropriate transitions) onto an *edit recorder* VCR. The sound on the original videotapes can be copied 'straight', or 'lifted off', prepared separately, and 'layed back' as a new soundtrack.

Hours   Mins   Secs   Frames

Time code

During videotaping, exact data is recorded that allows every instant to be identified. This is used for cuing and editing. The time code can be displayed within the picture, or read out on a separate indicator.

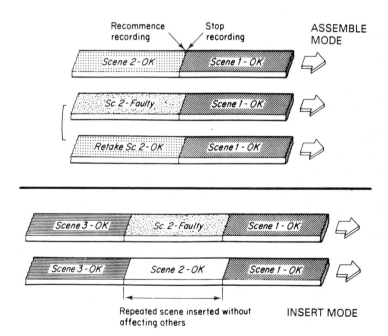

Videotape editing

Assemble mode: A further scene can be *added* to an existing recording; to replace faulty shot, or add new material.

Insert mode: Here the new material is recorded *within* the recording. This method avoids interrupting the system's synchronizm (control track pulses).

169

Electronic Insertion

Using electronic wizardry, you can punch a 'hole' or *matte* in a *master* shot, and
insert there the exactly corresponding area of a *background* picture.

Keyed insertion
The *SEG* (*special effects generator*) is usually part of the *switcher* facilities. It
automatically interswitches between pictures to produce:
- *Uncover wipe patterns* – removing a section reveals another shot.
- *Split-screens* – subdividing the frame, to show parts of two shots.
- *Insets/inserts* – displaying a section from another shot, within the main
picture.
   You can select various adjustable geometrical shapes, with hard or soft
(diffused) edges, and position them anywhere in the screen. A variation on this
method uses a silhouette graphic placed in front of a supplementary camera, to
provide the matting. You can make this *camera matte* any shape, and
expand/contract it by zooming.

Chromakey (CSO)
Wherever blue appears in the *subject/master shot*, this system automatically
switches to the *background scene* from another video source instead. So a
person in front of a blue surface appears 'inserted' into the other shot. The
background scene itself can contain any colors.
   You can create elaborate 'multi-layer' effects or 'multiple images', by using
this composite picture as the 'background' for other insertions.

Take care
If you are not careful, though, strange effects can develop:
- *Limitations.* Anything moving outside an 'inserted' area will be *cut off* or
vanish. Chromakey subjects normally move *in front of* the background shot.
- *Background breakthrough.* Occurs if the hue you are using for switching
(usually blue) is worn or reflected by the subject.
- *Incongruities.* Incorrect scale, wrong proportions or perspective, ridiculous
situations (e.g. standing in space).
- *Accidental effects.* Both foreground and background cameras' shots must be
held still. Panning/tilting causes 'flying'. Zooming causes growing/shrinking.
- Some chromakey systems will insert cast shadows of the subject. In others
shadows cause spurious breakthrough.

Typical applications
- To insert a closeup shot within the main picture.
- To imitate a wall display screen, or a window in a setting.
- To place a person 'within' a photographic background or model.
- To use photographs, artwork, models (miniatures) as the background for
action, instead of built settings.
- To create scale changes such as giant animals, tiny people, growing/
shrinking.
- To produce magical effects such as appearances/disappearances (total or
partial), people flying or falling from a height.
- To form 'living paintings' in which you brush the canvas with the keying hue
and the subject appears.
- *External keying* circuits insert 'solid' titling into pictures.

170

ELECTRONIC INSERTION

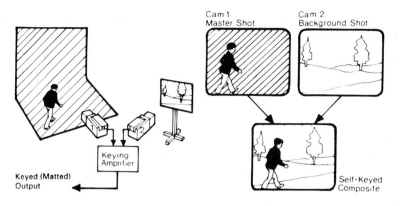

Using chromakey
The master Camera 1 sees the subject in front of a blue background. Wherever the keying amplifier 'sees' blue in the shot, it switches to the background picture on Camera 2. When combined, the subject appears 'in' the background shot.

Insets
Part of one shot can be inserted into another, by using a simple *corner wipe* – hard or soft-edged.

171

Guiding the Talent

How much guidance talent needs, depends on several factors:
- Are they used to appearing in public?
- Are they speaking impromptu, or working from a learned script, or reading a prompter?
- Are they giving a performance or acting?
- Is the action complex? Do they have to work to floor marks, and take cues?
- Will they be on their own, or continually aided?

Inexperienced talent
You may need to do no more than welcome people, and outline what you want them to do. But don't expect too much of the inexperienced. They may not do the same thing twice! Keep their problems to a minimum. They need reassurance and self-confidence, so wherever possible, support them with an experienced *host/anchor-person*.

Don't overburden people with instructions. When necessary, explain how to present items to the camera; but don't give them elaborate things to do. Don't rearrange or change anything if at all possible. It only confuses. Do make it clear whether someone is to speak only to the host, or to address the camera (and which one). If talent is to move around, indicate where they are to stand, and check that they understand.

People who are not used to TV studios find activities around them distracting and worrying. Sometimes you can strengthen their confidence by positioning a small *cue card*, listing points they are to cover, beside the camera. But inexperienced people reading from scripts or prompters are usually unnaturally stilted and ill at ease.

Where somebody who lacks TV experience demonstrates a process or equipment, they will often appear more spontaneous (and predictable) if they explain it to a host/anchor-person, who can guide them by questions, and make sure that cameras can clearly see what is going on.

Experienced talent
People who are very familiar with studio routine keep cool under the most trying conditions, remaining in command of the situation, whatever happens around them. They take the FM's hand cues (or prompts) from the corner of an eye. Many wear an *earpiece*, which is relaying the director's comments, suggestions, information about program timing, or changes of plan . . . and respond without an eyebrow's twitch although on air! They can stretch or reduce material, or improvise as the need arises.

General points
Try to avoid the uncertainties of under-rehearsal, or the tedium of over-rehearsal. If the next item is not ready, rehearse something else meanwhile, rather than allow interest to fall off through inaction. Otherwise have a definite stand-down, with a specified return time.

Rehearsed interviews or discussions lose spontaneity. Sometimes you can rehearse the show outline, using substitute questions/ topics as a 'warm-up'. Otherwise, it's best to use stand-ins in the planned positions to line up shots, and run through the show's mechanics.

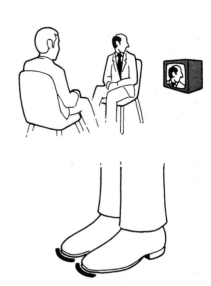

Watching monitors
A nearby monitor can be a strong temptation for a person to watch himself!

Toe marks
Chalk or crayon marks around feet, show talent their rehearsed position when there are no locating points.

Locating points
A person may be located by a piece of furniture – to ensure accurate positioning of shots.
Within a setting, they may use various scenic features as locating points as they move around.

Cuing

A cue is given to start or to stop action – to indicate when to speak, to move, to operate equipment, and so on. This requires careful timing; in anticipating the right moment, and judging how long the recipient will take to respond.

If action or dialogue is cued *too early*, it will begin before the shot is ready, or before it has been selected on the switcher.

When cued *too late*, we cut to a shot, and then see the action spring into life!

If you cue the next item *late*, you can leave the previous performer on the screen after they have finished their contribution . . . bewildered and unsure whether to ad lib or just grin. In a live show, wrong cuing can result in your audience seeing film or videotape leaders, or in the inserts running out and leaving a blank screen!

Forms of cuing
- *Word cues* are agreed 'go-ahead' points during dialogue, commentary, or discussion, to cue action (a move, or an entrance), or to switch to an insert. *Out cues* or *out words* are the word cues at the end of a filmed or taped insert.
- *Hand cues* given by the FM are a standard method of starting studio action. Where the talent cannot see the FM, the cue may be relayed – occasionally a tap on the foot or shoulder may be necessary.
- *Monitor cues* are taken from watching action on a studio monitor, and beginning commentary or action at an agreed point (e.g. as a car door closes). A few seconds *run-in* and *run-out* picture (without dialogue) is used as a *cushion (buffer)* at the 'top' and 'tail' of any film or VTR insert. A *time-cue* is a countdown from a cue-point, before commentary or action begins.
- *Light cues* may be taken from the *camera tally (cue) light*, which comes on as the camera is selected. Small portable *cue lights* can be used (for announce booths, or actors waiting behind scenery). The standby 'flick', followed by a steady 'action light'.
- *Buzzer cues* are used in some areas (film or videotape to production control room), e.g. one buzz 'Yes' or 'Start', two buzzes 'No' or 'Stop'.
- *Talkback cues* are given direct to a performer such as a newscaster or sports commentator wearing an earpiece.
- *Clock cues* are go-aheads at a specific time.
- *Electronic cue-dots* appear as small black/white squares or circles in the corner of the transmitted picture at network program-change points, say 30 to 10 sec and 5 to 0 sec.

Film cuing
Film is set up in the projector (telecine) at a chosen cue-marked point. On starting the machine, the first required picture frame then appears after a known delay, e.g. 4 sec. So if the machine is started about 12 words before the switching point, studio dialogue will stop just as the 'in-frame' appears. The cue-mark may be a sync-numeral on a standard film leader (e.g. 4) or a marked frame. (An 8 sec. 25 word cue may be used.)

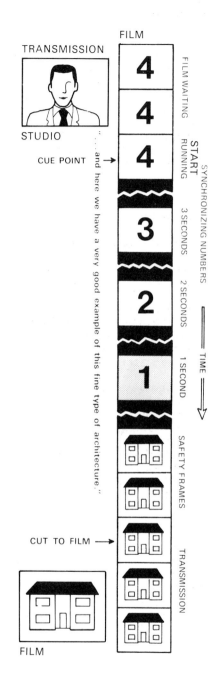

The principles of film cuing
The film is laced up, projecting the chosen synchronizing number. (This represents a known run-up time.) At the cue point in the speech, 4 sec before it is due to finish, the projector is started. The film machine runs up to speed.
Precisely 4 sec later, the film pictures begin.
Safety (Buffer) frames allow for slight timing leeway.
As the speech ends we cut to the film, and its picture is transmitted instead.

Prompting

When someone extemporizes, you can't be certain what they will say, or how long they will speak for. It's far more convenient if they can work to a scripted dialogue – which, in most cases, has been written by someone else. But how do you ensure that someone is going to deliver this script?

Approaches to presentation
- *Reading to camera from a script.* Seldom really effective. The reader often looks preoccupied, stilted and unnatural.
- *Working to notes.* Often successful for experienced speakers, but liable to variations.
- *Learned script.* Even an actor who is used to committing long passages to memory may not have time to learn the lines.

Sometimes you can get round the difficulty by having someone read a 'voiceover' commentary to the pictures.

Forms of prompting
To ensure that there are no errors or omissions, you can help talent in several ways:
- *Corrections.* When someone 'dries' (forgets the next word or topic), or 'fluffs' (makes an error or says the wrong thing), or 'cuts' (leaves out material), a quiet word prompt or a note may be sufficient to restore matters.
- *Reminders.* A list of points to be made, or topics to be discussed, can be a valuable *aide-memoire* – whether pencilled on a demonstration table, or displayed on a nearby chalkboard.
- *Script boards* are often used by commentators/interviewers/presenters/ anchor persons. Their various notes, questions and research work are attached to a clip board, and form their reference point. Some find this approach too interrogatory, and prefer small cards or palmed notes.
- *Cue cards (goof sheets, idiot cards)* held near the camera, or suspended on rings beneath *(flip cards)*, can display reminders – e.g. of song lyrics.
- *Electronic prompter ('teleprompter').* This is the sheet anchor of many TV shows today! The performer reads the entire dialogue 'spontaneously' from a continuous rolling copy of the script at or near the camera lens. Earlier prompters used paper rolls displaying 'jumbo type' text, but nowadays, electronic versions are universal.

The performer looks at the camera lens, but sees reflected in an angled glass a copy of the script displayed on a picture tube. Designs vary, but typically this remotely controlled image presents lettering around 15 mm (⅝ in) high, with some 20 words visible in an 8-line frame.

The trick is to read it naturally, without a fixed stare, 'casually' moving your head to disguise eye movements. The camera's distance and height may need to be adjusted to allow the prompter to be read easily.

Prompting – direct methods
1 Handwritten prompt cards, usually held near the camera, may contain dialogue or reminder notes.
2 Camera flip cards usually carry brief reminders.

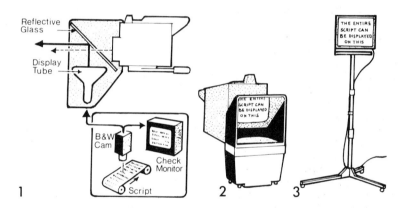

Video prompters
1 Video prompters use a 45° clear glass sheet at the camera lens, reflecting a picture-tube display of the script from a nearby script-scanner (monochrome TV camera shooting a miniature roller script), or a computer-stored script. Simpler prompters reflect a wide paper roller script with 'jumbo' type.
2 The camera lens shoots through the glass sheet at the subject. The reader appears to be looking straight at the lens and the audience. (Other systems can result in an off-camera stare.)
3 Where the speaker does not need to speak directly to the camera the prompter-script video may be fed to floor video prompters or monitors.

The Commentary

Since the earliest days of sound film, the *commentary* has been a familiar device in news stories, travelogues, demonstrations, sports events, and public ceremonies of all kinds.

The commentator's role
In most programs, the commentator is an observer or informant; explaining the events we are watching. Although usually unseen (VO – voice over; OOV – out of vision), the speaker may also appear in shot from time to time.

Scripted commentary
Scripted commentaries are usually written to accompany program material which is not self-explanatory, and usually without dialogue. It is a particularly useful way of joining together a series of apparently unconnected shots. (Music can also do this, but leaves the viewer to work out what is happening.)

A well-written, well-read script sounds like spontaneous conversational observations; not like a prepared speech. The scripted commentary is carefully timed to fit the recorded picture. If there is insufficient time for some essential information, the picture sequence may be extended (built out, stretched) to last long enough (e.g. by adding, repeating, slow motion, etc.).

It is annoying when introductory comments are made *too early* – leaving us waiting for the event. But even more frustrating is information that *lags behind* the action we have already seen!

Unscripted commentary
Here the commentator, armed with researched information on the subject, speaks spontaneously. A good commentary *supplements* a picture, and does not overwhelm it. That's not always easy when it's an exciting sporting event, and tension is growing. There's a tendency to describe what the audience can see for themselves. An experienced commentator neither states the obvious (e.g. she is getting out of the carriage), nor insults the viewer's intelligence (e.g. he is about to put the loaf in the oven to bake). Yet it happens! A good commentary draws attention to those visual clues that the less well informed viewer might have overlooked or forgotten. The technique is to *identify* which player it is with the ball, or the problems of the game, rather than *describe*.

There will often be prearranged *out-cues* agreed with the director for any cued-in inserts (e.g. film or VT clips, titling, photo-stills). This avoids the embarrassment of the commentator referring to insert items that are not ready to show!

If surroundings are noisy, use a fairly close microphone with a wind shield or a noise-cancelling mike. And always speak a few words as a *level check (voice test)* before recording, for the audio engineer to adjust equipment.

Cuing
Commentators use several forms of cues, including:
- Hand signals from the FM.
- Intercom cues from the director.
- Word cues (e.g. from an announcer).
- Monitor picture cues (. . . and here he is!).

Out-of-vision commentary
Where the commentator is never seen, he may be located in an announce-booth, or in a corner of the studio.

Desk monitor
Where the commentator is seen in shot at a desk, a small monitor may be hidden within it, unseen by the camera.

In-shot monitor
A nearby monitor shows film or videotape on which the studio talent comments. Where a color monitor is used in shot, it requires careful color re-balance for it to look correct on camera.

179

The Single Performer

Many regular television formats pivot around a single performer: as a presenter, host, introducer, commentator, master of ceremonies, anchor, demonstrator, lecturer . . .

Relationship with the audience

The performer can relate to the audience in various ways:

- Looking straight at the camera, addressing the viewer.
- Doing a job, but looking up periodically to speak to camera.
- Working at something, while ignoring the camera. (There may be commentary over – either the talent's or prepared script.)
- Speak to someone out of shot (usually near the camera).
- Work to a studio audience, and ignore the cameras.

It is important that the performer knows which approach is appropriate. Sometimes, of course, it will vary during the production. If they are to speak to a camera, they should know which. (Usually the one with the red *tally light/cue light* illuminated.) It may be necessary for them to know exactly where and when to stand, sit, or move, and the limitations of the shot (especially for closeups of held items).

If the performer is following a prompter, avoid rigid stares, anxious peering, or furtive glances, by making sure that:

- They have read the text beforehand (preferably they have written it).
- They have no difficulty in reading it at the camera's working distance.
- They know the prompter will keep up with them (an operator controls it to suit the reading rate).
- They know the tricks of random head/eye movements and expression changes, to disguise the reading action.

Action

Keep action simple, particularly if the talent is not familiar with TV mechanics. Make it clear *when* you want the talent to move. The FM can give a series of separate cues if necessary.

Some directors have the talent continually moving around . . . standing, sitting, walking, leaning, gesticulating, turning to new camera viewpoints to provide visual changes. It looks fidgety; the result of discomfort rather than technique! The secret is to make changes appear rational and naturally motivated. Certainly don't just let the talent wander around at random, but give them definite location points.

Shots

Head-on static shots are dull. Try to introduce camera movement (dollying/tracking) or zoom changes from time to time, to vary interest, to emphasize points, or to change concentration. Occasionally, the camera might arc round from a frontal to an over-shoulder shot; but take care that such a move does not look laborious.

Let someone know when his actions will affect your shots. Don't *assume* that because he happened to hold the jar during rehearsal so that we could read the label, he will do that on the air. Show him the problems, and if necessary, how he can check the shot on a nearby picture monitor.

Angling the desk
Straight-on frontal or side views can look posed and awkward. Instead, angle the desk slightly.

Subject movement
The performer should not be kept in a static position for too long. But in moving and repositioning him, always consider whether the result is appropriate.

181

Interviews

This is probably the commonest type of situation on TV, and appears in one form or another many times a day.

In the studio
While guest(s) are being received, the director is setting up shots in the studio, and briefing the crew.

Typically, 'stand-ins' (e.g. crew) sit in the chairs while shots, lighting and sound are checked. Chair positions are marked on the floor (chalk or tape). The guests take their places, and chat with the interviewer while the sound engineer checks voice levels. Camera operators should look out for any signs of idiosyncrasies; any tendency to lean back or forward, make wide arm movements, etc.

Directors have different approaches to interviews:
● Discussion before the studio, then a single recorded take of the required duration.
● A long continuous take, from which highlights are extracted.
● A take of the required duration; retaking unsatisfactory sections.
● What is virtually two separate interviews with a break between, the final show being edited from them both.

The method adopted may be varied to suit the temperament of the guest, how quickly they settle down, whether there are repetitive or uninteresting passages, etc., and the time available.

Rehearsal can produce spontaneity. While it gives confidence to some, it causes others to omit, repeat or change information. Some guests need patient coaxing; others are hard to stop.

Ensure that the guest has seen in advance any film or tape inserts being referred to. It is often best if nearby picture monitors show only these inserts. Many people find shots of themselves distracting or preoccupying.

Location interviews
An inexperienced guest feels most at ease when interviewed at their home or work place. Studio surroundings seem artificial and unfamiliar.

One regular technique is to have the interviewer out of picture (unheard), while the camera concentrates on the guest − zooming to vary the shot. Wherever possible avoid lengthy interviews with a hand-held or shoulder-supported camera.

After the interview is complete, you can take:
● Two-shots of guest and interviewer, as the latter repeats the questions.
● 'Nod shots' of both the guest and the interviewer (usually imitating the smiles and head-nodding of an attentive *silent* listener).
● Shots of the interviewer repeating the questions to the guest (confirming them from an audio check-tape if necessary).

These shots can be inserted into the program at appropriate places, to allow editing to remove any unsatisfactory sections, and to trim the interview to the exact length needed. At the same time, these 'cut-ins' will disguise camera position changes, or breaks in the conversation, and create variety.

When someone cannot get to the studio, the solution may be to show them on a picture monitor, or a panel insert in the interviewer's picture.

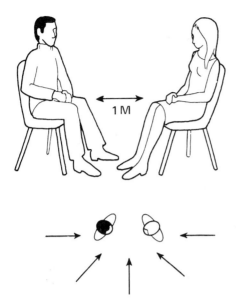

Talent positions
If people sit within about a metre (yard) of each other an optimum variety of
shots becomes possible. More widely spaced (page 101) and frontal two-shots
are impracticable.

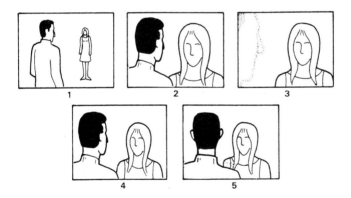

Over-shoulder shots
The proportions of over-shoulder shots are important.   1. Too distant.   2. Too
similar in size.   3. Too close. These are rarely satisfactory.   4. A slightly angled
front person (nose just visible) is preferable to a back-of-head view, 5.

Talk Shows

All talk shows follow a common theme: a group of people sitting in formalized arrangements, talking. The programs themselves may vary from a panel game to a press conference, from a discussion group to an audience quizzing a group of experts. But the production treatment is similar enough.

Controlling the program
Names abound for the person who is guiding and controlling what is going on in front of camera – aided by the director's intercom earpiece instructions, and the FM's signals: Presenter, Anchor person/Anchorman, Chair person/Chairman, Link-man, Master of Ceremonies/Emcee (MC), Host, Interviewer, Coordinator, as well as the more specialized assignments such as Announcer, Sportscaster, Commentator. . . .

Like the interviewer, this person needs research briefing, to be familiar with the production's aims and details. He/she will guide discussion, be aware of time allowances, and introduce the topics and the guests/participants to the viewer. The 'presenter' controls discipline, by encouraging one person to speak at a time, preventing undue dominance, steering discussion back to the subject, maintaining it along the planned lines. The presenter's particular talents reach their zenith when there is an on-air crisis, for then they will anticipate problems, improvise, stall . . . anything to keep the show running smoothly.

Layout
The layout for a talk show usually consists of a series of chairs or desk setups, arranged perhaps on a low platform (rostrum) in front of a cyclorama or series of scenic flats.

Groups of chairs tend to look unattractive; particularly in longer shots. On the other hand, more casual seating such as sofas and armchairs are cumbersome, and make shot continuity and grouping more difficult. So the practice of using scenic 'desks' evolved. These 'dress up' the presentation, and add a sense of occasion or formality. They keep people close together, and avoid the 'forest of knees' effect seen on camera when shooting lines of chairs.

Typical shots
In talk shows, intercut single closeups, two-shots and group shots are the regular diet; with the occasional overall view (cover shot), and perhaps a *cross-shot (side shot)*, or *over-shoulder shot*. Because sustained pictures of individuals soon pall, the director will usually intercut reaction shots of different members of the group. These can help to establish a feeling of rapport (or antipathy!) between the speakers. But do avoid the vacant gaze, and the preoccupied or disinterested look – unless, of course, that is appropriate comment! 'Reaction shots' showing hands nervously tapping or the fingers intertwining with anxiety are easily overdone.

In some situations, people speak in an agreed order. But in an *ad-lib* discussion, it may be prudent to have one camera continually taking wide shots, to give you a picture to cut to, while another camera seeks a closeup of the new speaker.

Layouts

Layouts for talk shows can be arranged to provide *individual impact* (people in chairs), or to create *segmented unity* (people are divided into sections), or to present *group unity* (in an assembly). The interviewer (I) or chairperson/link/anchor, has a coordinating role. Each layout has its particular convenience and adaptability. Desks add formality or a sense of occasion.

185

Newscasts

News presentation on television has evolved over the years, until today it follows a pretty standardized form throughout the world:

- Narration to camera (from a prompter).
- A series of brief videotaped or filmed stories.
- Live-action video inserts (usually remotes/OBs).
- Graphics with the reporter's voice when there are no pictures.
- Live topical studio interviews.
- Illustrative graphics (charts, maps, etc.).
- Titling from character generators (identifying subtitles, quotes, etc.).

This format is also used for other 'omnibus'-type programs. In *sports round-ups*, for example, a central sportscaster will introduce a series of live, filmed or videotaped items and interview guest celebrities.

General setup

The newscaster reading the prompter reflected at the camera lens appears to be speaking directly to the viewer. There is usually a script on the desk for emergencies (and to give authenticity to the spoken word), but direct script reading is avoided wherever possible.

An *earpiece carrying intercom (switched talkback)* from the director and news editors prepares and cues the newscaster for upcoming stories. *Picture monitors* show:

- The on-air transmitted picture.
- A preview picture of the *identification clock* (VTR) or *leader* (film) for the next story.
- There may also be a *cue light*, which can be operated by the director, to indicate when to begin speaking.
- A nearby desk telephone enables the newscaster to contact the director in an emergency.

Behind the newscaster's desk, many TV stations use a relatively plain background, displaying a station logo and a frame identifying the current story. This frame may be rear-projected, but is usually an SEG electronic insert, or a chromakey patch. When an *in-shot* picture monitor is used as a display screen, it can also be utilized for remote interviews.

The TV cameras (which may be remotely controlled) seldom move, but zoom to adjust the shot size.

Basic organization

Good presentation relies on careful organization. An up-to-date running order is essential, including last-minute items and deletions, *in-cues* and *out-cues* and durations for each section. Program timing can be affected by the speed and accuracy of the newsreader's reading. Timing cues in the prompter script can assist in keeping the dialogue in step with the picture, introducing pauses of appropriate length wherever necessary. *Ad libs* may not be welcome, particularly where precise cuing is being taken from prearranged word cues.

To anticipate possible failures (e.g. film breakage, problems with a satellite link), it is usual to hold timed *reserve stories* on a standby VT or film machine. The newsreader has suitable announcements at hand.

186

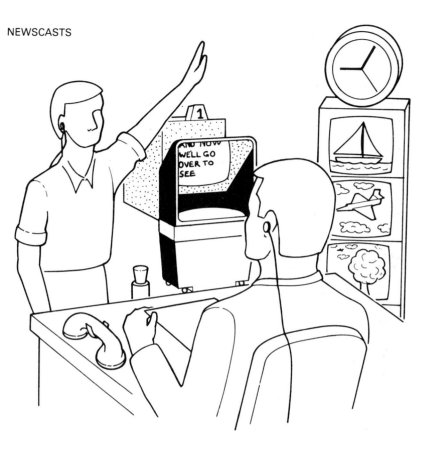

As the newscaster sees it

Although apparently at ease talking directly to the audience, the newscaster is in reality working to a carefully timed presentation surrounded by various aids: prompter, picture monitors, clock, floor-manager, standby script, cue-light, desk phone to director.

187

The Illustrated Talk

Illustrated talks are a very economical and flexible method of presenting a wide variety of program subjects.

Gathering material

The most obvious approach is to go out and shoot subjects as a documentary. If your program is discussing an industrial process, you may take a video camera along to a suitable factory or works, to shoot the subject in action. This may be quite practical, but it is not necessarily the best solution.

Firstly, there are often practical limitations:

- The cost, time, travel and general organizational effort involved.
- Local distractions, intrusions and noise can interfere with location shooting.
- All the required subjects may not be available.

Quite often, shooting on location reveals a lot less about the actual process than a good diagram would achieve!

The most effective, interesting illustrated talks are often composite programs, bringing material to the studio in the form of film and video clips, photographs, slides, graphics (diagrams, charts, graphs, sketches), models, and specimens.

Some productions rely on an *expert* who is at ease with TV production mechanics to handle the subject. Others have an experienced TV *presenter* working from a prompter script written by experts – discussing items with an expert guest; providing commentary, while the director explores the source material with the cameras.

Typical staging formats

There are several regular formats when presenting this type of program:

- A *neutral* non-associative setting – e.g. a cyclorama background to photo blowups, decorated flats, screens; and tables/benches, graphics, wall-charts, models.
- An *atmospheric* setting – e.g. suggesting a study, library, hobbies room, workshop.
- A *locational* setting – suggesting a laboratory, factory, museum.

Whatever the style, aim to make the decor visually interesting; but not over-decorative. A 'show-biz' presentation lacks authenticity.

Presentation hints

- Avoid over-cluttering the setting with items that are never seen properly.
- Over-shoulder shots looking down at hand-held items can be awkward to shoot – camera position; hands obscure details; shadows; cannot get close enough.
- For closeups of items, place them on a prearranged table mark. Check the shot on a nearby monitor. At certain angles, light reflections may bleach out details.
- Instead of holding an item up to camera for detailed closeups, it is usually better to edit in detail shots afterwards; or cut away to a duplicate on another camera or a slide.
- When showing book illustrations, use *page markers* to avoid fumbling or wrong selection. (Don't tantalizingly show pages that will not be seen properly!)
- Simplify all graphics. Keep labeling, long lists and statistical tables to a minimum, and don't overcrowd the screen.
- Remember, close shots of poor photographs or newspaper clippings do not always reveal more detail.

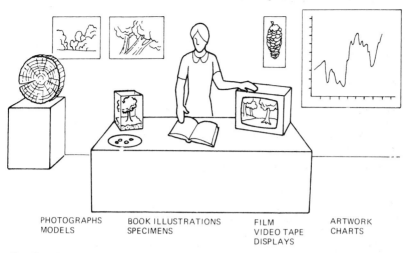

PHOTOGRAPHS   BOOK ILLUSTRATIONS   FILM   ARTWORK
MODELS   SPECIMENS   VIDEO TAPE   CHARTS
                                              DISPLAYS

Studio talk

The production is a composite of recorded material interlinked with studio presentation. The camera explores specimens, models, illustrations, graphics, etc.

The illustrated talk on location

A talk 'on location' (real or reconstructed), illustrates fashions, using paintings, book illustrations, a girl in period dress, etc.

189

Demonstrations

A good demonstration doesn't simply *display*. It arouses curiosity. It intrigues.

Organizing demonstrations
Here are some important practical points to look out for when arranging any demonstration:
- Above all, consider your audience. Who is the demonstration for? Is it to be a general survey, or to discuss a particular feature? Do you need to simplify, or can you rely on their having certain knowledge and experience already?
- Don't try to cover too much in a single program. It is easy for information to become too superficial, or too congested.
- Remember the old maxim: 'Outline the program topic – Tell them about it – Then give a summary of the main points'.
- Wherever possible, have one section lead on to the next. If there are several isolated topics, have visual bridges (graphics/titling) between them.
- When organizing items to be demonstrated, get full details about such factors as dimensions, weight, supply requirements (power, water, compressed air), expendable materials needed, safety precautions necessary, process durations, transportation problems, insurance, etc.
- Always check apparatus on arrival, and before/after use. Make sure it is carefully collected and returned or stored.
- Try to arrange items in a consecutive sequence, rather than moving to and fro between them.
- In a bench demonstration, reduce visual clutter by removing (or keeping out of shot) anything you've finished with (e.g. dirty dishes, previous items).
- A demonstrator preoccupied with mechanics may not be able to follow a prompter. So words and durations can vary between rehearsals and takes. When a program's duration is critical, it may not be easy to cut items if it overruns, or 'pad out' if it underruns. To simplify editing, consider including extra 'cushion'/'buffer' sequences that can be expanded, shortened or dropped to suit the scheduled duration.
- A long demonstration can become boring to watch. Rather than show it all, include examples of each step of the process, or make a start-to-finish recording, and show just its important stages (a particularly useful approach for unreliable processes!).

Demonstrations in closeup
To assist focusing and framing when taking very close shots:
- Begin with a longer shot before cutting to detail. (This shows relationships and scale.) When in doubt, go to a wider shot, and insert detailed closeups during editing.
- Don't continually zoom in and out on details. It's irritating to watch. Camerawork is unsteady when zoomed in to detail (focusing; shake).
- Don't put things in and out of an empty shot.
- Keep the demonstrator's hand movements slow and restricted in close shots. It may be better to use a pointer or a pen to indicate fine detail, than point with a finger.
- Check for distortion, shadowing, or light reflections.

190

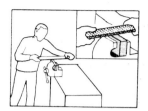

The inset
An inset enables us to show detail and overall effect simultaneously.

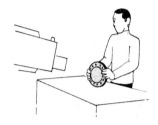

Working to the camera
Whenever possible, the demonstrator should work to the camera.

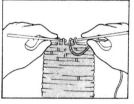

Camera viewpoint
Sometimes the demonstrator cannot work to the camera. Aim to get the best viewpoint available in the circumstances.

Comparisons
To compare situations, a split screen can show before and after conditions.

191

Music and Dance

Some directors choose shots 'spontaneously'; others carefully analyze the performance beforehand. But in the end, the way you stage and shoot music and dance is mainly influenced by the *purpose* of your program.

Approaches
● *If your aim is effect*, then you will probably use light to engender mood – dynamic camera movements and ever-changing compositional patterns to enhance musical structure; slow mixes, fast cutting, superimpositions to echo the tempo.

● *Where the presentation is more formal*, emphasis is on clarity, with the camera concentrating on performance and techniques, rather than dynamics.

Sometimes a particular presentation technique may be used for quite different purposes. *Slow motion*, for example, can be used to convey a dreamy, languorous mood, or simply to show more clearly the details of fast movements.

It's important to choose the right *transitions*; quick cutting for fast sequences, gradual mixes perhaps for slower ones. They must be precisely timed to suit music and action.

Occasionally you may use a soft-edged inset, or even a superimposition, to show detail (a soloist) within a general view. But take care that visual gimmicks do not distract from the performance.

Particularly when shooting *dance*, the secret is to be in the right place at the right time! Long shots show us the overall pattern of movement. But are we missing an individual performance that can only be seen in a closer shot? While concentrating on the particular, are we losing the overall impact?

When presenting *music* (bands, orchestras, groups), it is essential to shoot instruments from appropriate angles. A very narrow lens angle can distort and compress subjects together. Getting the right shot from the right position, at the right moment, is no mean feat! It needs careful attention to the score, precise planning, and skilled camerawork. There's nothing more frustrating than cutting to an instrumentalist just as he's finished playing – or seeing the wrong instrument!

The soloist
Soloists (singers, instrumentalists) can be presented in innumerable ways. Their background might range from neutral to abstract; from a decorative treatment to a realistic environment. In *location* shots, soloists usually perform (mime) to tape playback, while walking beaches, wandering in countryside . . Occasionally, instead, a series of atmospheric shots (e.g. library film) are used to accompany the performance.

Pop music
Visually, anything goes – all the video effects tricks, speed changes, electronically doctored images, multi-images, quick cutting, bizarre lighting! The aim is to be *different*; to intrigue, amuse, astonish, shock. Glitzy visuals may make even mundane material arresting.

192

Closeups
Closeups of performers may be informative, but not particularly attractive.

High shots
High shots can reveal overall pattern and team formations.

Ground shots
Ground shots can show footwork, steps, swirling skirts.

Isolation
When shooting within a group it may be impossible to isolate individual performers so that unwanted items or people appear in shot.

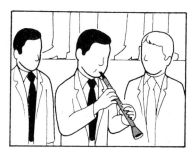

193

Quiz and Game Shows

By now, you will have recognized how some show formats share common features. There are, for instance, basic similarities between an *illustrated talk* and a *demonstration*; although the practical emphasis is different. You will find that the staging and camera treatment for most 'quiz shows' bear a close resemblance to those we met earlier for 'talk shows'.

Game shows
Here the contestants compete individually or in teams, to carry out tasks of some kind — from party tricks to acrobatic feats. They are usually working against the clock.

The usual arrangement is for contestants to enter, and stand at certain prearranged positions, where they are questioned by the MC or quizmaster. They then go to meet their particular challenge.

There are variations on this theme, but typically, the main action areas include:
- The entrance.
- The 'interview area' where the MC greets the contestants.
- A display area with gimmicks to operate or select, subjects to name, etc.
- The scoreboard and/or a countdown clock.
- The prize area.

If the staging area is fairly limited, you can arrange lighting in an overall 'three-point' pattern, with a single main key light, balanced against soft light from the other direction, and appropriate back lights (the scenery being lit separately). When the action is more widespread, treat the various action areas separately.

The sound pickup arrangements depend on what is going to happen. Occasionally, you might be able to get by with just a single hand mike held by the MC, pointed to contestants in turn. But in most situations you will need more comprehensive arrangements, such as a sound boom, wireless mikes, or operators pointing shotgun/rifle mikes.

Quiz shows
In most quiz shows, the contestants are seated behind some form of desks. The MC/quizmaster may walk around, or be seated behind a similar desk. The shots and lighting are essentially as in a 'talks' setup, with desk mikes or persona mikes for sound pickup.

Organization
The MC is the central figure in the show: friendly but firm, and totally impartial Using answer cards, a timing sheet, or intercom guidance, he keeps a brisk pace and controls the running time.

In order to check shots before recording, it is useful to have a brief 'rehearsal with 'dummy questions'. This helps the contestants to overcome their initia nervousness, and allows lighting, sound and makeup to be checked with the actual people involved.

Typical shot allocation

Most quiz shows tend to follow a similar style format. Consequently regular shooting patterns develop. Where the contest is between two panels, with the chairperson as adjudicator, the panel shots are duplicated.

195

TV Drama

Television drama today spans productions from Shakespeare to 'soap operas'; from the highly stylized to the totally naturalistic. TV drama at its best blends the influences of script, performance, camerawork, scenic design, lighting, sound treatment and editing . . . to produce results that the viewer accepts as 'reality'!

Film and TV drama
There are essential differences between the potentials of *television* and *film* drama.

In most *motion pictures*, shots alter rapidly. Emphasis is on action, changing activity, varied environment. The image on the large screen of the movie theater tends to dominate its audience, who have a strong sense of involvement. The large screen is excellent at presenting the broad effect, and imparting an awareness of location.

In *television*, the restrictions of the small screen affect the home audience's reactions. They tend to scrutinize or inspect. (Spectacular effects are invariably diminished when shown on the TV screen.)

The smaller and more intimate nature of the TV screen concentrates the attention and gives emphasis, in a way that could appear grotesquely over-blown on the larger screen. The most effective television studio drama is slower paced, emphasizing the interplay of human relationships, character development, and people's reactions.

TV drama techniques
There are several productional approaches to TV drama:
● In a widely used multi-camera method, the cameras are strategically positioned, and move very little from these viewpoints – typically center and either side of the set. (Where necessary, action is adjusted to suit the cameras.) The size of shots is varied by altering zoom-lens' angles. Cameras' pictures may be fed to a switcher, or taped on *dedicated VTRs*.

This productional method is easier to plan and direct, and makes fewer demands on the production crew. However, it can degenerate into a mechanical routine in which the director arranges the action, and then selects whichever camera happens to have the best viewpoint!
● Another multi-camera method uses a more dynamic approach. Action is systematically planned to achieve particular compositional effects; usually with the aid of storyboards. Camera viewpoints are mobile and continually varied to suit the action. Cameras move in amongst the action (developing shots). Clearly this technique requires careful organization, and skilled operation. Editing may be immediate (production switcher), or post-production.
● Another approach is to shoot the production on a single video camera (*rehearse-record*) in a 'shot-by-shot' filmic fashion. The camera is totally mobile All editing is carried out during post-production, together with audio sweeten-ing (adding effects and music), electronic effects treatment, etc.
● It is possible to shoot studio drama with a single video camera, using chromakey or reflex projection systems to provide backgrounds to the action These backgrounds can originate from photographs, slides, film or videotape artwork or computer graphics.

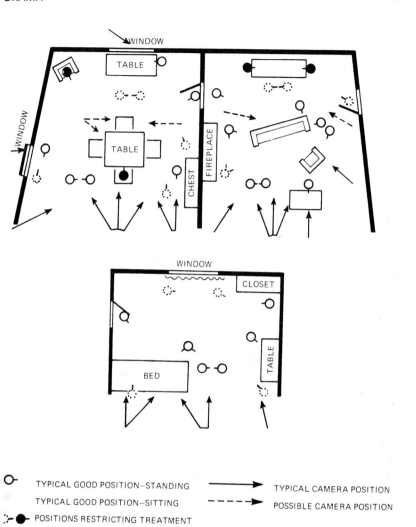

TYPICAL GOOD POSITION–STANDING   TYPICAL CAMERA POSITION

TYPICAL GOOD POSITION–SITTING   POSSIBLE CAMERA POSITION

POSITIONS RESTRICTING TREATMENT

Basic room layouts for drama

The architecture and furnishing layouts of rooms directly influence the action-patterns and shot opportunities. Some positions offer better shots than others. Most action is central and downstage, taken on cross-shooting cameras. This provides maximum shot opportunity, and minimum audio and lighting difficulties.

The Studio Audience

Unquestionably, certain productions gain appreciably from the presence of a studio audience. Comedy shows, in particular, lose their 'edge' when played 'cold' to the camera. Even an appreciative camera crew's reactions can help.

Controlling the audience

Various audience conventions have evolved. At concerts, for example, we expect our audience to be silent except for subsequent applause, hopefully not coughing, fidgeting, or reacting audibly. In 'situation comedy' shows (comedy action in realistic settings) we want to *hear* the audience laughing and clapping throughout, but not whistling or giving inaudible smiles. They are not seen on camera, though, for this would disrupt the 'real-life' presentation.

Because long laughter can slow down the show, upsetting timing, the FM diplomatically but firmly encourages and terminates audience reactions. He, or the director, has explained this need during the welcoming *warm-up* before the show with smiles, jokes, or other encouragement.

Some studios use applause signs. Others introduce recorded applause, usually during editing/dubbing sessions afterwards, to augment or substitute for the audience. Directors argue that although recordings may seem unethical, and often sound phoney, at least they are controllable!

Effect on performers

Some directors contend that talent can time their laughs and business better to a studio audience but others feel that the tempo slows, relative to the home viewers' more rapid reactions. When talent is unused to TV work, they are more inclined to 'address' the audience, or use a 'stagey' delivery, instead of the more confidential, intimate approach that is more suitable for TV.

We may find our studio audience reacting to events that the camera is not yet showing (a clown awaiting his entrance). This can puzzle and frustrate the home viewer. Studio audiences are also liable to over-react, due to group enthusiasm, determination to enjoy themselves, and a rather less critical attitude than the isolated viewer.

Accommodating the audience

As well as providing comfortable, safe seating, we must ensure that our audience can see the studio action clearly. So sets have to be arranged facing them, slung picture monitors and loudspeakers helping them follow the television treatment.

When audiences actually participate in the show, cameramen normally offer reaction shots, that the director intercuts with the front-of-camera (or on camera) material. But if people see themselves on monitors, we must be prepared for giggles, and shy and extrovert behavior. Self-consciousness ruins reaction shots.

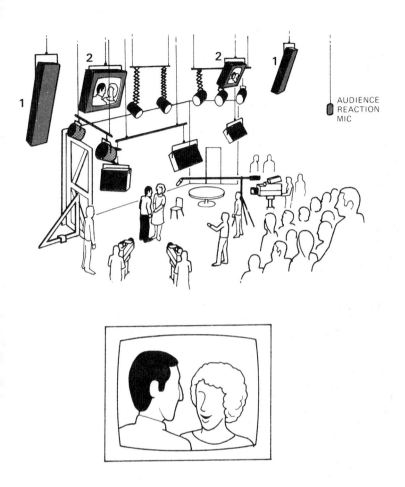

AUDIENCE
REACTION
MIC

Studio audience viewpoint
The studio audience watches a performance under intriguingly unfamiliar
conditions, with distracting mechanics all round. 1. Foldback loudspeaker.
2. Picture monitor. The viewer sees nothing of the behind-the-scenes activities,
and is quite oblivious to them, seeing only a naturalistic, 'real-life' situation. The
various floor operations (e.g. close cameras) should not obscure the action from
the studio audience.

Reminders on Effective Directing

There's a great deal of pleasure and satisfaction in working on a well-run TV production. But a lot depends on how effectively the director organizes and handles his team. Let's try to summarize typical factors that encourage effective teamwork.

- Plan your show. Even a basic outline aids coordination.

- Get very familiar with your script beforehand, so that it becomes a reference point, not a crutch.

- Have firm ideas. Don't begin a rehearsal with vague hopes, or an expectation that it will be 'all right on the night'. Don't rely on multi-takes during videotaping, in a hope that eventual editing will cobble together a worthwhile production.

- Welcome your guests, and ensure that they know what you want them to do.

- Get to know your team beforehand. Don't just accept them as 'facilities'.

- Some directors call crew members by name, instead of by function. On balance, it prevents ambiguities to refer to 'Camera 1, Boom, Lighting' – particularly when they are all named Joe!

- Always check that all the studio team, and contributors, e.g. film, VTR, can hear intercom (talkback), and are ready to go.

- Be constant when using terms. Use local terminology.

- Give clear guidance. Be decisive. Be firm but friendly, but don't order or browbeat. It does nothing but demoralize. Critical observations that are acceptable face to face create tensions when heard over intercom (often without the opportunity to reply!).

- Continually scrutinize preview monitors – Are shots OK? Any guidance or changes needed? Have cameras moved to their next positions? Are graphics/titles ready and OK?

- Rehearse from the *production control room*. Don't keep going into the studio to alter or correct. It wastes time, and concentration lapses. Most problems can be rectified from what you can see on camera, and with the aid of your FM and those members of the crew concerned.

- Ensure that the crew knows which section you are about to rehearse (setting, shot number). If you are going over a section again, check that people realize why, and what was wrong last time.

- Check at intervals on progress relative to available rehearsal time.

- Don't leave items unrehearsed. Always check at the end of each section that the crew is ready to go on to the next.

- Give preparatory standby to any source that has not been used for a long period, such as film inserts, or he may not be ready for immediate cuing.

- Tell performers if they are creating problems, e.g. he is shadowing her, or his hand is in the way. Don't assume they know, and will correct.

200

- Some situations are not readily transformed by 'doctoring', e.g. loud music cannot be faded down to make it a 'quiet background' behind commentary. A light-toned scene cannot be made to look dark by exposure or video adjustment (only by careful lighting treatment). Hence a daylight photograph cannot readily be transformed to 'night'. A dark-toned setting cannot be made to look light, however strongly lit.

- If there is a delay during rehearsal because, for example, an item is not ready, pass on to another item, checking the linking between later.

- After a rehearsal, have a short break to discuss with the performers, and the crew if necessary, any points to be corrected.

- Be punctual. Don't be late starting rehearsal; time is precious. Don't leave people hanging about, waiting and wondering what to do. Always break at scheduled times such as meal breaks, and announce return times, and the point from which rehearsal will recommence.

- Always be prepared to cope with a breakdown of facilities – particularly on live transmission – and anticipate possible alternative arrangements such as substituting another camera.

- Do not over-rehearse – particularly amateur or inexperienced talent. It produces uncertainty, woodenness, less dynamic performances. Do not use time just because it's there. Under-rehearsal is equally undesirable.

- After videotaping, hold the studio until the recording has been checked. If retakes are necessary, make this clear, and announce the sections and shot numbers involved, what was wrong, and the order of re-recording. Consider any costume/make-up/scenic changes necessary for the retakes.

- At the end of transmission (taping) thank the crew and the performers. Be ready to praise work well done – but don't gush. They are professionals and know when they have done well or badly. A kind word oils the wheels of progress. Don't hold post mortems!

Rehearse/record

- There are advantages in shooting with a single camera, rehearsing, then immediately recording the action: less detailed planning; no camera coordination problems; immediate retakes of errors; opportunities for rethinking, improvisation, improvement; less elaborate facilities needed during shooting – only during post-production editing.

- Disadvantages include: tendency to less disciplined shooting (unnecessary multi-versions for later selection); instant correction needed for any shortcomings/faults in lighting, scenery, costume wardrobe, makeup etc. is very time-consuming; intrinsic problems in continuity of action, lighting, sound, etc.; considerable 'post-production' work needed on editing, audio, video correction, effects, etc.

201

A Check List of Common Errors

A lot of things can go wrong in any TV production. We notice them and put them right if possible. In the brief lists that follow, you will see the sort of problems various members of the production team are looking out for. Some are important, others slight. But they all affect the overall quality of the finished product.

Control room
- Picture monitors inaccurately adjusted (color, brightness, contrast).
- Picture monitors don't show all of picture area ('overscanned').
- Light falling onto picture monitors (diluting picture color and contrast).
- Sound monitoring unsatisfactory (too loud, too soft, poor quality).

Performance errors
- Unconvincing, 'wooden', 'mannered', out of character.
- Lines vary from script. Sections missed.
- Wrong positions, not on floor marks, wrong moves, action, timing.
- Wrong business, items handled incorrectly.
- Working to wrong camera.
- Voice too loud or too quiet.
- Fidgety, inconsistent, late on cues.

Camera errors
- Focus not sharp, focused on wrong subject (or at wrong distance), losing focus (i.e. not following focus on moving subject).
- Missed shot (not on shot at the right moment). Wrong shot (size wrong; wrong subject; wrong angle).
- Poor composition (wrong framing – headroom excessive or insufficient; subject position in frame wrong; subject cut off). Composition not as rehearsed.
- Camera out of position (off its floor marks).
- Unsteady camerawork (wavering shot, unsteady dolly movements, unsmooth zooming).
- Poor panning or tilting (not following subject smoothly).
- Wrong camera height.
- Wrong lens angle.
- Caught readjusting (shot taken while adjusting focus, zoom, height, etc.).
- Over shooting/shooting off.
- Lens flares.
- Incorrect color correction for prevailing light.

Lighting
- Too flat (subject lacks modeling).
- Too contrasty (over-dramatic for situation).
- Inappropriate lighting angle (too steep, too angled for subject or situation).
- Important subjects or areas cannot be seen.
- Areas too bright (artistically unsatisfactory; overexposed).
- Excess back light.
- Unattractive or inappropriate pictorial effect.
- Unrealistic or incompatible lighting treatment (e.g. phoney night, poor fire flicker).
- Distracting reflections.
- Distracting 'technical' shadows (shadows of camera, mike or boom, bystanders, equipment, etc.).
- Distracting 'artistic' shadows (on people or background).
- Artistically inappropriate shadows or light patterns.
- Unattractive portraiture (inappropriate, emphasizes facial defects, ages).
- Poor environmental illusion.
- Poor pictorial continuity from different angles, or between shots.

Scenic treatment
- Unconvincing or inappropriate treatment.
- Design lacks visual appeal.
- Design not suitable for shots used (e.g. ineffective in close shots).
- Design restrictive – only suitable for certain viewpoints.
- Extravagant design. Identical effect could have been achieved more easily or cheaply.
- Scenic treatment and/or layout restricts cameras, lighting or sound.
- Surface tones or finish create problems (e.g. too light/dark, shiny).

202

Video control
- Pictures under- or overexposed.
- Picture contrast excessive or insufficient.
- Highlights too bright.
- Shadows too thin or dense.
- Poor color balance.
- Poor matching between successive pictures (in color or contrast).

Inserts (film, video, slides, graphics)
- Poor 'technical' match to studio pictures (quality, color values, brightness, contrast).
- Poor 'artistic' match to studio pictures (continuity, ambience, pace, etc.).
- Distracting blemishes (scratches, dropout).
- Sound out of sync (e.g. voice to lip movements).
- Slides of poor quality (bad color, blemishes, unsharp, misaligned).

Titles
- Too large, small, misaligned, crowded, poorly framed.
- Inappropriate type face (artistically or technically).
- Unsuitable tones or colors for the background.
- Titling and background confused, too similar.
- Consecutive titling unmatched.

Program sound
- No sound.
- Opening or closing works/notes missed (late fade-in or early fade-out, tape editing fault, poor cuing).
- Unwanted sounds heard (early fade-in or late fade-out, tape editing fault, poor cuing).
- Extraneous sounds (sound channel wrongly left faded up).
- Performer sounds too distant (wrong mike faded up, poor mike position, talent in wrong place).
- Performer sounds too close (wrong mike faded up, poor mike position, talent in wrong place).
- Poor sound balance between sources (relative loudness of sounds inappropriate, background sounds too loud, scale or proportions of sound do not match picture).
- Inappropriate acoustics (e.g. reverberant open-air shot).
- Extraneous noises (air conditioning, movement of equipment or crew, camera cable drag, equipment noise, hum, script pages, costume rustling, footsteps, doors, moving/adjusting settings, rumble of wind on mike, etc.).
- 'Hollow' sound (distant mike used, wrong phasing, feedback).
- Sound effects don't match picture.
- Unsatisfactory sound quality (incorrect tonal balance).
- Audio defects (clicks, crackles, hum, tape dropout, speed fluctuations).

Editing
- Wrong shot (wrong camera, wrong take).
- Wrong transition (e.g. cut instead of mix).
- Poor transition (mix too fast or slow, badly balanced super, hesitant wipe).
- Late or early cut (action missed or duplicated).
- Poorly matched action.
- Cutting rate/rhythm inappropriate.
- Unsatisfactory cutaways/cut-ins (irrelevant, poor match).

Makeup
- Inappropriate (exaggerated, insufficient, style).
- Worn (patchy, requires renewal).
- Perspiration (shiny skin).
- Hair needs attention (dishevelled, wig/hair-piece attachment).
- Corrective makeup needed (skin tones, defects).

Clothing
- Inappropriate (style, tones, fitting).
- Clothes need attention (dishevelled, creased, dirtied).
- Unsatisfactory tones (too light, too dark, shiny).
- Unsatisfactory color, pattern, or finish.
- Damage (torn, unstitched).
- Causing sound problems (noise with personal mike).

Shooting on Location

On location, you have to be self-sufficient, prepared to improvise and to cope with prevailing conditions – from weather to power failures.

Types of location unit

Anywhere outside the confines of the studio is a 'location'. You may be shooting anything from a brief program insert (e.g. street interviews), to an entire production. It may be a multi-camera *remote (OB/outside broadcast)* covering events staged by someone else (e.g. a parade). Or it could be an *EFP/electronic field production* that you are initiating – drama perhaps.

The facilities necessary can vary considerably. Depending on the scale of the production, you may need anything from just a single camcorder unit, to a full-scale remote unit with mobile studio facilities, microwave links or satellite dish!

Preparations

Success begins with efficient site reconnaissance – the 'recce'. Careful planning and anticipation at this stage can avoid many headaches later. After a preliminary investigation, the director and his specialist team check out details.

To give you the flavor of this project, let's list just a few of the points to look out for:

Interiors:

- How much space is available? (Small areas restrict the longest shots.)
- Are there viewpoint restrictions – e.g. pillars, stairs?
- Any problems with acoustics – e.g. clap your hands to detect echoes.
- Any extraneous sounds – e.g. creaking floors, traffic?
- Views outside windows obtrusive – e.g. busy street?
- Natural room lighting (daylight/artificial) satisfactory? Will it be when you shoot?
- Do interior furnishings need readjustments, augmenting?
- Any major changes needed – e.g. block off window?

Exteriors:

- Weather problems. (Consider what to do if it's unsuitable.)
- Consider possible lighting problems on the day of the shoot – e.g. light reflectors, diffusers for strong sunlight; booster lamps for dull day.
- Any extraneous noise problems – e.g. traffic, aircraft, animals, machinery?

As you can see, a lot depends on whether you are shooting for a short time, or over some hours; whether you can use existing daylight, or will need a full lighting rig; whether your shots are localized, or taking in a large area . . .

Organization

You need to take a very practical approach to location production.

The right facilities can help to make the going smoother – e.g. a mobile phone, radio intercom, loudhailer.

It is particularly important to anticipate any possible editing difficulties: perhaps by shooting more than one version of the action (straight retakes, or variations), taking 'cutaways', recording sound *wild tracks*, taking reference photographs for continuity or studio matching.

Checking out the location

When you are choosing a location to shoot, there are a number of factors you may need to look into. Information that may seem trivial at the time can affect your entire project.

DEFINE LOCATION
- Map/route/distances/travel time.
- Sketch site layout.

WEATHER
- Weather predictability?
- Shelter available?
- Precautions needed?
- Alternative shooting possible?

LEGALITY
- Local permission needed?
- Fees, gratuities payable?

ACCESSIBILITY
- Easy access at all times?
- Traffic problems?
- Parking problems?

SAFETY
- Protective clothing?
- Dangerous situation?

INHIBITING FACTORS
- Local restrictions?
- Others working nearby?
- Equipment operating nearby?
- Public access?
- Crowds likely?
- Local holidays?

SELECTING VIEWPOINTS
- Best camera positions?
- Good visual coverage?
- Positions easily reached?
- Safe?
- Any obstructions?
- Unwanted features visible?

LOCAL NOISE PROBLEMS
- Tide, wind, waterfalls . . .
- Low aircraft, traffic, machinery . . .
- Animals, birds, school . . .

AID NEEDED?
- Need local advice?
- Need local guidance?
- Need local assistance?
- Police, fire, hospital?
- Is item locally organized?
- Inform local residents?
- Local labor needed?
- Locals as performers?
- Local transport needed?

FACILITIES
- Power, water required?
- Local facilities hired?

WELFARE
- Accommodation needed?
- Feeding arrangements?
- Personal comfort?
- Security arrangements?
- First aid?

TRAVEL
- Transport of performers, crew?
- Transport of equipment?

SCENERY/PROPS
- Scenery, props required?
- Transport of scenery, props?
- Labor for erecting/dismantling scenery?
- Labor for set-dressing location?

MAKEUP/COSTUMES
- Transport of makeup, costumes?
- Makeup facilities?
- Changing facilities?
- Storage/security arrangements?

LIGHTING
- Equipment needed (lamps, cables, etc.).
- Transport of equipment?
- Supplies, cabling?
- Labor for rigging and operating?
- Lighting control arrangements?

SOUND
- Equipment needed (mikes, cables, etc.).
- Transport of equipment?
- Supplies, cabling, control?
- Rigging and operation?
- Sound control arrangements?
- Playback required (miming)?

INTERCOM
- Methods of intercom needed?
- Methods of cuing?

DIRECTION
- Production control arrangements?
- Picture and sound monitoring?
- Single or multi-camera shoot?
- Switcher or post-production edit?
- Review, off-line editing?

VIDEO CONTROL
- Picture control facilities?

VIDEORECORDING
- Location or base VTR?
- Using camcorder, VCR, VTR?

Color

Color brings a picture to life; engendering moods, suggesting subtle nuances of style. Color associations are endlessly varied.

Color has its practical aspects too. It can arrest interest, direct attention, help to clarify detail and differentiate between areas.

Color can be *subtle* (diluted, desaturated, pastel hues), or *blatant* (bright, pure saturated hues). Excessive color can be overwhelming. While certain color relationships are comfortable together, others are vibrant; some clash violently.

Colour is subjective

Unless color reproduction is particularly bad, we tend to assume that it is 'natural', 'realistic' – 'just like everyday life'. We accept colors in a picture . . . untill we happen to compare them with another version nearby. Then we ask which is 'right'!

As we look around, eye and brain continually adjust, arbitrarily interpreting color and tone in ways the camera cannot. We get *impressions* that are quite untrue. Shoot the same colored dress against different background hues and brightnesses, and the dress color we 'see' will appear to change with each. We may prefer one version to another; yet neither may be accurate.

Color is different on the screen

We react to 'compositional' effects on the flat screen that simply *don't exist in the actual scene*. A picture may show a distant flagpole 'growing out of someone's head' – yet no-one on the spot sees this effect!

Our impressions of color on the screen are very arbitrary, and can depend on:
- The subject's surface (rough, smooth, shiny), angle, brightness.
- The subject's background color and brightness.
- How much of the frame the color occupies.
- Predominant colors in the previous shot.

Comments on color

- Our impressions of screen color can depend on our viewing conditions (ambient light, local decor).
- When isolated within the picture frame, colors tend to appear more intense than in real life.
- Superimposed shots can intermix hues, to produce new colors (deliberately or accidentally).
- Color easily appears brash, garish – cheapening visual appeal.
- A small area of color can dominate the screen in closer shots; yet appear incidental in longer shots.
- A limited area of color has strong attraction when seen within neutral surroundings.
- Even when defocused, background subjects in color can distract. In *monochrome* TV, their tones merge unobtrusively to overall gray.
- Color details are lost in more distant shots. Small areas of color can merge to produce a different hue.
- Large areas of red reproduce with pronounced picture noise.
- Intercutting between shots of the same subject gives an immediate visual comparison, revealing differences in their color quality ('mismatching').

Color mixing
1. *Mixing light* – When colored
light beams are intermixed
('additive') they form new
secondary colors. In equal
proportions, they mix to *white*.

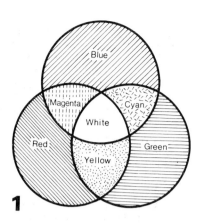

1

2. *Mixing pigments* – When
magenta (red–blue), yellow,
and/or cyan (blue–green) inks,
paints or dyes are printed onto a
surface ('subtractive mixing'), new
hues develop where they overlap.

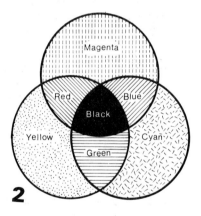

2

Color harmony
In this color circle, complementary
colors are opposite. 'Triads' that
harmonize together (e.g. green,
orange, purple–blue) are
separated by 120°. In practice,
harmony depends on the colors'
relative saturation, brightness,
area, finish, etc.

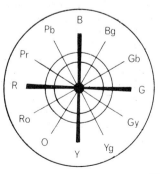

207

Appendix – Calculating Shots

If you want to plan a production systematically and predictably, a transparent lens-angle (or protractor) laid on the *scale staging plan* is a fast and effective technique. It shows you at a glance exactly what you are going to see from any viewpoint, whether you are likely to be shooting off or getting another camera in shot. As you go through the scene, you can mark the camera positions on the plan as a record for eventual rehearsals.

However, you will meet occasions where you need the solution to an isolated problem, and do not want to resort to measurements on squared paper. This graph can help with its summarized information. It will show you the lens angle and distance needed for any standard shot, as well as subject proportions in the frame.

How to use the graph

1. Follow a vertical line from your camera distance to the lens angle in use, and *the shot you get* is shown on the left.
2. Similarly, you can see *how far away* the camera needs to be for a particular shot. Locate your shot on the left, follow across to the lens angle used, and the distance is below.
3. What *lens angle* is necessary for a shot? A horizontal line from the shot type joins a vertical from camera distance, at the lens angle you need.
4. The scene *width and height taken in* are shown in the left-hand column, so you can see camera distances required.
5. *Proportions*, too, are shown. If a subject is to occupy one-third of the screen width (or height), multiply its actual width (or height) by three (or whatever proportion is involved), and use the vertical width scale to deduce the distance from your lens angle.

Lens angles

The corresponding horizontal and vertical angles covered are;

Horizontal	Vertical
degrees	
5	3.75
10	7.5
15	11.25
20	15
25	18.75
30	22.5
35	26.25
40	30
45	34
50	37.5
55	40.25
60	45

UNIVERSAL CAMERA SETUP GRAPH

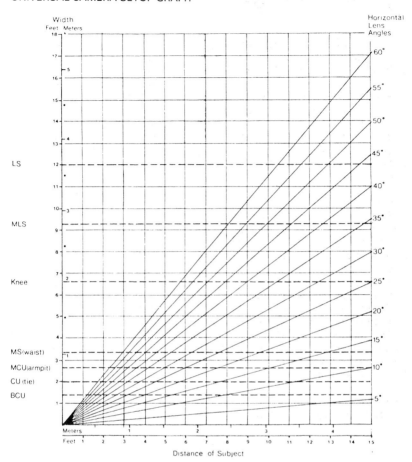

The graph shows direction and staging details that would otherwise need continual measurement. It is calibrated in feet and meters, but can be interpreted in inches. To use it for greater distances multiply the scale readings by a similar factor (e.g. × 5).

Further Reading

If you want to explore further aspects of television/video production in greater detail, the following companion books by Gerald Millerson are available from Focal Press.

The Technique of Television Production, 12th edn.
An established standard textbook used in universities, broadcasting organizations, TV and film schools throughout the world. This is a detailed practical discussion of the mechanics, techniques, and aesthetics of the medium. It explains the power to persuade and the nature of audience appeal.

Video Production Handbook, 2nd edn.
This realistic, practical guide to low-cost video program-making explains how to achieve professional standards with limited facilities and a restricted budget.

Video Camera Techniques
A quick lucid guide to the essentials for handling video cameras.

The Technique of Lighting for Television and Film
An internationally established sourcebook, discussing in detail the principles and techniques of the art of lighting.

Lighting for Video, 3rd edn.
A rapid guide to practical lighting techniques in video and television production.

TV Scenic Design Handbook
A study in depth of the art, mechanics and techniques of scenic design for television and video production.

Glossary

Acting area The area within a setting where action takes place.

Action line (imaginary line) An *imaginary line* connecting two subjects. If shots from cameras on either side of this line are intercut, the direction of action and performers' positions will be reversed *(reverse cut)*.

Action props Articles ('properties') used specifically during performance; e.g. pipe, knitting, wallet, gun.

Actor A performer, usually in a dramatic role, portraying a particular character, and speaking scripted dialogue.

Additive mixing Mixed in various proportions, the color primaries of light (red, green, blue) can produce all hues in the visible spectrum.

Address A particular point in a videotape recording, identified by the associated time code.

Ad lib Unrehearsed, unscripted action or speech.

Asymmetrical balance Pictorial arrangement in which a larger object close to the center of the screen is balanced by smaller object(s) near the screen edge.

Background *Scenic:* Areas appearing behind a subject. *Also* the picture inserted into a *chromakey* shot. *Audio:* Sounds kept at a lower volume, behind the main subject sound (e.g. traffic noise). *Program research:* The underlying facts; information on which program material is based.

Backing Scenic planes (flats, backdrops) outside a window or door, suggesting areas beyond; and preventing cameras overshooting the setting.

Backing copy (protection copy) Duplicate audio or video recording; in case the main copy is faulty or becomes damaged.

Back light Light directed towards the camera; used to outline subjects in light, separating them from their background, creating a three-dimensional effect.

Balance To adjust relative intensities (of concurrent sounds or light sources) for an artistically satisfying effect. Hence *pictorial balance* relates to the distribution of line and tonal masses in a picture. *Sound balance* relates to the relative prominence of sound sources.

Blocking Working out the performers' positions, moves and action, relative to the cameras' positions.

Blocking rehearsal (dry run) A rehearsal of all action in a scene (often without dialogue). Either in rehearsal rooms, or in studio before camera rehearsal.

Bloom (block off, crush, burn out) An excessively light surface reproduced as a blank white area. (Due to overexposure or hitting system's limits.)

Blowup Greatly enlarged photograph.

Boom, sound An extensible tubular arm holding a microphone at its end, and supported on the central column of a wheeled base.

Burn in (burn on) Titling or timecode information that is 'solidly' imposed on a picture. *Also* An image of a bright area retained (permanently or temporarily) on a camera tube, defacing subsequent pictures.

Business Arranged activity, usually introduced to give conviction to a performance, or to give time for an operational move (e.g. pouring coffee, while a boom swings into position).

Busy An over-decorated, over-complicated, or elaborate effect.

Camcorder A camera with either an integrated or attached (dockable) VCR unit.

Camera tower A demountable tubular tower, used to support a high camera.

Camera trap A specially arranged opening within scenery (e.g. sliding panel, hinged wall-picture) through which a concealed camera can shoot into a setting.

Canted shot (canted angle) A shot tilted sideways for dramatic effect.

Cast Actors/performers seen and heard in a production. Hence *cast list*.

CCD (charge coupled device) A solid-state light sensor used to convert the lens image into a video signal. (Increasingly replacing the *camera tube*.)

Chain General term for a complete assembly of technical equipment with a specific function; hence *camera chain, audio chain*.

Character generator (CG) Device with a 'typewriter' keyboard, used to electronically generate titling (letters/numbers), which can be inserted directly into the television picture. May provide multiple fonts, selectable sizes, storage (files), graphics generator, etc.

Chaser lights A series of small lamps automatically switched in sequence, to give the impression of light movement.

Chromakey/CSO Electronic equipment for inserting a 'subject' with a color background (e.g. blue) into any video 'background'.

Clapperboard An identification display board ('slate', 'board') held in front of the camera at the start of a take. Its hinged clapper (clapstick) is slapped down, to enable picture and sound to be synchronized accurately during editing. (Data displayed includes title, take no., reference no., director, etc.) When shown at the *end* of a take, the slate is held upside down.

Clip A short section excerpted from a film or videotape; usually to become an *insert* into another program. *Also* To inadvertently omit a note, syllable or word from the start or end of a sequence.

Closed circuit Not transmitted/broadcast. A program fed (distributed) to limited selected points.

Colorize Using electronically generated hues to color a monochrome picture; e.g. provide colors in black and white titles.

Color temperature The color quality (spectral distribution) of light; varying with the nature of the source. Daylight has a high color temperature (measured in *kelvins*). Candlelight has a low color temperature. As a tungsten lamp is dimmed, its color temperature falls. The video or film's *color balance* (proportions of red, green, blue) should match the light's color quality for maximum color fidelity.

Contrast The relative 'brightness' of lightest and darkest tones. Hence 'high contrast' (extreme tonal differences), and 'low contrast' (little difference between tonal variations).

Costing Cost assessment of materials, equipment, labor, etc.

Cover shot A wide, overall shot of the action.

Crane, camera A special type of camera dolly with a counterbalanced beam (jib, crane arm, boom) on a wheeled platform. Camera height can be adjusted over an appreciable range, depending on design (0.45–8.2 m/1.5–27 ft). *Also* 'To crane' is to move the crane up/down.

Crash zoom A very rapid zooming action.

Credits Names of the production team and cast, at the start/end of a program.

Crop, to To cut off. A shot framed (deliberately or accidentally) so that it omits subjects near its borders.

Cross-cutting Continually interswitching between two or more camera viewpoints.

Cross-fade A mix/dissolve. Fading out one source, while fading in another.

Cross-shot A shot from an oblique viewpoint.

Cushion Potentially expendable program material, that can be shortened, or cut to adjust the overall program duration.

Cutaway A separate shot introduced within a main action sequence, to deliberately interrupt its continuity (e.g. a crowd shot during a football game). Used to disguise mismatching shots, continuity discrepancies, etc.

Cyclorama/Cyc A continuous suspended cloth, providing a plain all-purpose background.

Dead Unwanted item. No longer to be used. 'Killed'. Not functioning ('dead circuit'). *Also* – Audio. Acoustic conditions where little sound is reflected (sound-absorbent surfaces).

Dedicated VTR Arrangement in which each camera has its own associated VTR in a multi-camera shoot.

Defocus mix During a mix between two shots, one camera defocuses, while another, which is defocused, sharpens on its shot.

Depth of field The distance range over which the scene appears sharp. It increases as the lens aperture is reduced ('stopped down'), with camera distance, and as the lens angle is widened.

Detail shot A shot showing particular detail (e.g. a silver mark), usually not otherwise clearly visible. (Often shot separately, and cut in.)

Digital video effects (DVE) Video effects created by storing the complete television picture in digital form, and then sampling this information selectively. It can be read out to produce segmentation, inversion, wipes, reversal, insets, magnification, reduction, multi-image screen, color transformations, etc.

Dolly A small wheeled platform that allows the camera to be moved around with precision. The camera itself is attached (via a panning head) to some form of tripod (*rolling tripod*), extensible column (*pedestal*), or movable jib arm (*camera crane*). *Also* a general term for any mobile camera mounting.

Dress, to To wear the clothes during rehearsal that are to be worn during the recording/transmission (hence *'Are they dressed?'* and the term *Dress run*). *Also* To arrange/position *set dressings* (i.e. ornaments, mirrors, drapes, furniture, etc.) to create a particular environment.

Drop out Momentary loss of picture or audio, due to imperfection or damage in magnetic tape's surface.

Dubbing To make a recording of an existing record (direct or modified copy).

Duplex/multiplex A mirror/prism arrangement allowing several projected sources (film, slides) to be directed to the same video camera (as in a *film island*).

Effects bus Row(s) of push-buttons on a switcher, combining sources for electronic effects including mixes, wipes, inserts, mattes, keying, etc.

Elevations Set designer's scale drawings, giving the dimensions and details of vertical surfaces – e.g. walls with doors, windows, surface treatment.

Establishing shot An overall shot used at the start of a scene, to reveal location, relative positions, etc.

Exposure Adjusting the intensity of the lens' image falling onto the camera's image sensor (CCD, camera tube) to obtain maximum tonal clarity in the subject – usually by altering lens aperture (stop) or lighting intensity.

Extender lens/Range extender An additional lens which may be flipped in or attached, to extend the zoom lens' normal range (increasing the focal lengths).

Favor, to To give greater emphasis to one rather than another ('Favor her in the shot, rather than him').

Feed, to To supply. Hence to '*feed* a monitor with Cam. 2's picture', or to 'feed him lines' (a prompt).

Flat A scenic unit made from a timber frame faced with plywood, compressed board, canvas. Made in various standard sizes, and used to form 'walls' of settings, and other vertical planes.

Floor plan Scale bird's-eye view of the layout of the studio staging area. Shows settings, furniture. Used as basis for all planning and technical operations.

Focal length The distance from the lens system's optical center (near nodal point) to the camera's light sensor when focused at infinity. Knowing this and the size of the sensor (CCD or tube target), one can calculate the lens angle. In a zoom lens, the focal length is variable over a certain range; e.g. 6:1 – a six times change.

Fly, to To suspend (scenery or objects). A digital video effect, causing an inset frame to move around the screen.

Foldback Sound played over loudspeakers near the action area. This can provide background sounds, or allow performers to hear music or effects (for cues or to accompany mime).

Freeze frame Arrested motion; by repeatedly scanning the same videotape or film picture.

Frontal shot A camera viewpoint shooting the action from a straight-on frontal position.

Gel General term for a colored material (plastic, gelatin) placed in front of a light source to produce colored illumination.

Generation Indication of how far removed a copy (dubbing) is from the *original recording* (the *1st generation*). Hence the first copy is a *2nd generation*, a copy of that is a *3rd generation*. With non-digital systems, there is a degree of deterioration in quality with each generation.

Gray scale A reproducing system's tonal range from white through to black can be subdivided into a series of equal tonal steps. The more steps that are clearly visible, the more subtle the reproduced tonal gradation. Around 7 to 10 steps is typical in TV pictures.

Hard focus Sharply focused. (Opposite of *soft focus*.)

Helical scanning (slant track) A universal method of recording video information on magnetic tape. As the tape passes round a sloping rotating drum containing the video heads, these record a succession of parallel slant tracks across the videotape.

Hue The fundamental color; red, green, blue, yellow, etc.

Indent clock (VTR clock, 'slate') Visual identifying data provided at the start of each recording, or 'take'. (Includes take no., scene no., date, etc.). It may be electronically generated, and include a countdown timer to the recording start, or take the form of a board with a clock display, held in front of a camera.

ISO (isolated) camera A separate VTR continuously recording the output from a chosen camera. During a live remote, this tape can be replayed into the program wherever necessary (for replay inserts, cover shots, or standby shots).

Lamp Strictly refers to an incandescent light source (e.g. tungsten lamp). Widely used to refer to an entire lighting fitting or luminaire. (Hence 'the background will need three lamps'.)

Lighting grid A pipework lattice fixed to the ceiling of smaller studios, from which lamps may be suspended.

Limbo Strictly, a totally neutral background for action; generally white.

Line monitor The main color monitor, displaying the source(s) selected on the switcher, to be recorded or transmitted. Also called *transmission*, *program monitor*, *master monitor*.

Line-up Technical adjustment of video and audio equipment, to provide optimum performance. May be carried out manually, or by automated circuitry.

Live Direct transmission of action as it happens. *Audio:* Reverberant surroundings.

Live-on-tape A production recorded from start to finish without stops or subsequent videotape editing.

Loop A length of audio tape or film in which the ends are joined together to provide continuous repeated performance: a repeat identifying announcement; a continuous effect (rain, fog).

M and E A soundtrack containing only music and effects. Usually prepared to allow dialogue tracks in different languages to be added later.

Magnetic track (mag track) Film sound may be recorded magnetically (single or multitrack): on a separate coated standard sprocketed film base (*sep-mag*), which is run in sync with the mute picture print; or as a *magnetic stripe* along the edge of the picture film ('married print'/'combined print').

Master control (central control) The central switching and engineering monitoring point in a studio center. All program sources (video and audio) are fed to master control – viz. remotes, VTR and telecine channels, production studios, etc., and routed to their respective destinations.

Matte (mask) A shaped area (physical or electronically generated) used to selectively combine two picture sources; one within the matted area, the other outside it.

Minimum focused distance (MFD) The shortest distance from the camera at which subjects can still be focused.

Mirror shot Picture in which the camera shoots a subject via a mirror, rather than by pointing directly at it.

Neutral Without associations. Hence *neutral tones* (whites, grays, black), *neutral settings* (plain, non-associative backgrounds).

Objective shots The camera looks at the scene, as an observer. (*See* **Subjective shots**.)

On-set graphics Graphics displayed within a setting. (*Off-set graphics* originate from slides, computer graphics, film, videotape, or are shot by a separate camera.)

Optical track A photographic soundtrack printed alongside the picture at the edge of the film.

Overshoot (shooting off) A situation in which the camera sees past the setting or a selected area, and accidentally reveals other subjects (e.g. overshooting the top of a setting, and seeing lamps).

Over-shoulder shot Shooting over the shoulder of a foreground person.

Pace The rate of emotional progression; *slow pace* (dignity, solemnity), *fast pace* (vigor, excitement). Derives from the dialogue, rate of delivery, action, editing, camera moves, etc.

Phasing Adjusting the exact synchronism of two signals. 'Out of phase' microphones result in hollow sound quality and volume variations. In video, *phase errors* cause color or positional inaccuracy.

Pickups A new shot in which someone speaking to camera uninterruptedly continues dialogue from the previous shot. *Also* any separate shot recorded after the main sequence, to be inserted during editing (e.g. 'detail shot').

Pixilation Jerky motion produced by regularly omitting some frames from continuous action. *Also* an animation effect obtained by conjoining a series of still pictures.

Platform (parallel, rostrum) A horizontal platform on a wooden or tubular frame.

Playback To reproduce audio or video tape for check purposes; usually immediately after recording.

Practical Able to work: scenery (e.g. doors) or properties (e.g. lantern) that function. *Non-practical* items (actual or dummy) appear convincing, but do not work.

Production van A mobile unit containing a television/video control room.

Properties (Props) Articles used to decorate settings; e.g. vases, books, furniture. *Personal props* are items specifically used or worn 'in character' by actors; e.g. a sword. *Action props* are used by a performer during the action; e.g. a flashlight.

Public address (PA) An audio system reproducing sound for a studio audience (program sound, announcements, music).

Public domain (PD) Non-copyright material that can be performed without permission or payment.

Reaction shot A shot of someone responding to the main action. The expression or gesture may be genuine or simulated. (Typically used in interviews.)

216

Replay insert During a live or live-on-tape program, an ISO camera's shots can be replayed in real time or slow motion, to repeat an action sequence (e.g. a goal scored).

Revamp To rearrange a setting or the set dressing, so as to change its appearance.

Reverse action Action made to appear backwards in time sequence.

Reverse cut A cut to another viewpoint, which shows the same action moving in the opposite direction. (The result of crossing the *action line*.)

Reverse shot A shot from the opposite direction to the previous viewpoint; e.g. from inside to outside a doorway.

Riser A small wooden block or platform (various sizes), used to support furniture and small items (for display, or to build up standard platforms – parallels, rostra). *Also* the vertical pieces between the steps in a staircase.

Roller caption Titling (e.g. credits) or other graphical material displayed on a long paper strip (usually black), which is rolled up the screen ('roll') or across the screen ('crawl').

Saturation The strength or purity of a color. *Desaturated* diluted with white.

SEG (Special effects generator) An electronic generator (usually part of the production switcher), producing a variety of geometrical wipe patterns, inserts, split screens, mattes, keys.

Selective focusing A technique for concentrating attention; by focusing on a particular subject, while others closer and more distant are left defocused (shallow depth of field).

Setting (SET) An arrangement of scenic units (flats, window and door units, pillars, platforms, drapes, etc.) to produce an overall scenic design.

Shot box Pushbutton facility on a TV camera, providing immediate selection of preselected zoom lens angles; often at a preset speed.

Shutter speed Electronic adjustment on a TV/video camera, controlling the sharpness of moving subjects.

Sit (set down, batting down on blacks) Electronically adjusting the video signal, to crush out the darkest picture tones to an even black.

Sky filter A graded lens filter, reducing the intensity or coloring of the upper part of the shot (to modify skies in that part of the picture).

Sneak in (or out) To introduce (or remove) imperceptibly, unobtrusively.

Soft focus Unsharp (accidentally, or deliberately for artistic effect). Opposite of 'hard focus'.

SOF Sound on film (i.e. on a film soundtrack); *com-opt (common optical), com-mag* common magnetic (i.e. magnetic stripe).

Special effects Any illusory visual effect. May be created optically, physically, electronically, by lighting, lens attachments, etc.

Specular A strong localized light reflection in a shiny/polished surface.

Split focus Focusing so that chosen subjects at different distances from the camera are equally sharply focused (i.e. distributing the depth of field between them).

Spread To take more than the allotted or anticipated time.

Stage brace An extensive prop or stay used to hold up scenery.

Stage hands Studio crew responsible for, for example, erecting scenery, mechanical cues (e.g. rocking 'moving' vehicles, handling camera title cards, etc.).

Staging The process of designing and arranging scenery within a studio; for maximum effect, and to allow optimum access for cameras, lighting, sound.

Staging area (setting area) The main area of the studio floor, in which scenery may be positioned. (Surrounded by a *safety lane/fire lane* from which scenery is normally prohibited.)

Star filter Inscribed clear disk placed over the camera lens to create rays of light around light sources or specular reflections.

Stretch To take more time, slow down, or ad lib, to fill the allotted time.

Strike To remove scenery, props, etc. from a setting.

Studio address/talkback The use of a loudspeaker system to address performers/staff in the studio.

Subjective shots Camerawork simulating the reactions of someone within the scene. (See *objective*.)

Switcher The *production switcher* is used to intercut or combine cameras and other picture sources in a multi-camera production. (It usually includes certain video effects facilities.) A *routing switcher* is used in Master Control, to route resources (studios, remotes, telecine, videotape channels) to their destinations.

Throw away To underplay a dramatic opportunity; either accidentally, or for deliberate effect.

Thrown, to be To be distracted, interrupting one's performance.

Tight Without surplus space around a subject ('tightly framed'). Running too close to allotted duration to permit 'spreading'.

Time code A system using a precise 24-hour digital clock, to show the instant at which each moment of the videotape was recorded. Used to exactly identify frames during editing. Normally laid down on a supplementary VT track during recording. Displayed when reproducing a VCR tape used for off-line editing.

Timing The duration checks that ensure a program keeps to schedule. *Also* Choosing the right moment and duration for an action (e.g. judging the pause before making a reply).

Title card A rectangular card supported in front of a camera. Printed on it is titling for show titles, credits, subtitles, etc., to be superimposed or inserted into shots.

Trim, to To aim and focus a spotlight: to maximum 'spread' ('fully flooded'), or minimum coverage ('fully spotted', 'pinned').

VCR (videocassette recorder) Videotape recording system in which the magnetic tape used is enclosed in a two-reel cassette. (*See* VTR.)

Video control (shading) Continual adjustment of video equipment by a shader/vision operator, to maintain optimum picture quality and match different picture sources. (Includes adjustments to exposure, video gain, black level, gamma, color balance.)

Voice over (VO) Dialogue from an unseen speaker (e.g. commentator) accompanying pictures.

VTR (videotape recorder) Videotape recording system in which the magnetic tape is wound on a single reel, and manually laced through the equipment, onto a takeup spool. (*See* VCR.)

Walk-through A preliminary studio rehearsal, in which performers go through basic actions and moves (without dialogue), primarily to show the studio crew (cameras, sound) the general form of the production.

Whip pan (zip pan) A rapid panning movement, completely blurring intermediate subjects.

Winging a show Unrehearsed direction.

Wipe To demagnetize an audio or magnetic recording. *Also* a transition, in which one picture is progressively hidden by another.